WISDOM
Is
BLISS

ALSO BY ROBERT THURMAN

*Available from Hay House
Please visit:

Hay House USA: www.hayhouse.com®
Hay House Australia: www.hayhouse.com.au
Hay House UK: www.hayhouse.co.uk
Hay House India: www.hayhouse.co.in

* * *

WISDOM
Is
BLISS

Four Friendly Fun Facts That
Can Change Your Life

ROBERT
THURMAN

HAY HOUSE, INC.
Carlsbad, California • New York City
London • Sydney • New Delhi

Published in the United States by: Hay House, Inc.: www.hayhouse.com®
Published in Australia by: Hay House Australia Pty. Ltd.: www.hay
house.com.au • *Published in the United Kingdom by:* Hay House
UK, Ltd.: www.hayhouse.co.uk • *Published in India by:* Hay House
Publishers India: www.hayhouse.co.in

Cover design: Barbara LeVan Fisher
Interior design: Greg Johnson/Textbook Perfect
Indexer: J S Editorial, LLC

Cataloging-in-Publication Data is on file at the Library of Congress

Hardcover ISBN: 978-1-4019-4343-1
E-book ISBN: 978-1-4019-4878-8
Audiobook ISBN: 978-1-4019-6320-0

10 9 8 7 6 5 4 3 2 1
1st edition, August 2021

Printed in the United States of America

To my Mothers,
*   who bravely create the miracle of life*
*   and caringly enable its infinite livability;*

To my Fathers,
*   who madly love them,*
*   and stand diamond true, in joyous awe;*

To my Lamas, the soul friends,
*   who open the door to the clearlight reality*
*   of blissful freedom and compassionate love!*

*   and*

To all my Children, every kind and hue,
*   the long now many coming generations*
*   on this magnificent planetary buddhaverse!*

May all the travelers upon the road
Find real happiness wherever they go,
And gain without needing too much struggle,
The highest goals which will fulfill their hearts!...
All of these practices were taught
By the Buddha for the sake of wisdom.
Thus those who wish to free themselves
From suffering must cultivate this wisdom.

—SHANTIDEVA (8TH CENTURY)

Don't try to use whatever you learn
from Buddhism to be a Buddhist;
use it to be a better whatever-you-already-are.

—H. H. THE DALAI LAMA

Contents

Preface

I love the Buddha, I really do. But I am not promoting the religion of "Buddhism" for anyone. I love just as much Ms. Buddha the Vajrayoginī, Her Holiness the Shekinah, the Great Mother, the blessed Moses, holy Mary, sweet Jesus, brave Khadijah, the holy Muhammad, wise Laozi, insightful Confucius, Radha and Krishna, Uma and Shiva, White Buffalo Woman, Wakan Tanka, Quetzalcoatl, Chalchiuhtlicue, countless shamanic teachers of indigenous peoples, and every single wise and loving grandmother—so many holy teachers, gods, and saints! They all perform such wonders and benefit so many, opening all kinds of amazing doors for all kinds of beautiful people, each to discover their own divine qualities, their wise intelligence and loving heart.

I do mention my beloved Shakyamuni Buddha more often, since I meet him more and more as I learn, discovering how helpful he has been to me—as a super-scientist, a super-educator, and a cool, global, social revolutionary; not so much as a spiritual person doing the great work of a religious prophet or a religion organizer.

I follow His Holiness the Dalai Lama's sincere policy and prime directive not to missionize or convert anyone from or to any religion or secular belief system. In fact, it is quite natural to stick to that policy, since the Buddha himself rebelled against the religions of his own time and, rather, set out to understand, rationally and experientially, the nature of reality.

The historical Buddha was a rigorous scientist, in the modern sense—that is, an explorer of reality. I also unequivocally declare that he is *the scientist* who successfully, accurately, and comprehensively discovered the "real reality," the miracle of bliss-void-indivisible freedom, yet for the sake of all the others did not ignore the less real realities.

Buddha was also an educator, so I try to learn and teach his curriculum, designed to enable any serious student of whatever faith or doubt to achieve reliable, lasting happiness. I have spent five decades doing university teaching *about* "Buddhism," somewhat mischaracterized as a "world religion" (since flat-earth, modern Euro-American philosophy departments have not yet discovered the "Pacific Ocean" of world-class, Buddhist and non-Buddhist critical philosophies). In this book I intend to teach the real thing, a buddha's threefold super-education, which is divided into eight branches.

Buddha had to be an educator, rather than a prophet or religion founder, since he had achieved his goal of an exact and complete understanding of reality by using reason, experiments to open his own mind, and death-transcending vision. He realized that since he, once a pampered yuppie prince, had been able to do it, other human beings also could do it. From his own experience, he could help them as a teacher by streamlining the process. He could not just transplant his realization into their minds. They could not get their own realizations just by believing whatever he said. He could only provide them with a prospect of full realization along a path of learning and experiencing they could follow—they would have to travel on their own. But we should never be discouraged; let's remember that he himself and all those who succeeded with his teachings over the millennia were originally just like you and me.

It is important to realize that the Buddha was not teaching "Buddhists," as there weren't any then. He taught all kinds of people who had grown up devoted to Vedist gods, Brahmin priests, and texts quite able to satisfy both mundane and spiritual concerns. Yet many of those same people were inspired by the Buddha's example and quickly found his teachings useful in their living practice. Many men and women were moved to enroll full time for his triple super-education—ethical, mental, and scientific— and they dropped out of their various life professions and became mendicant seekers, fortunately enabled to do so by the wealth and generosity of their societies. They were supported with "free lunch" scholarships by generous lay sponsors, kings and commoners alike. To keep it practical, they asked for brunch, not breakfast or dinner, and they vowed not to create their own families but to adopt all beings as their relatives.

I am not yet a buddha myself, but I am inspired by his example to trust that I will become one some day in the future, which will then be "now." Fortunately, he gave us a curriculum, which I have learned a bit about and will open up for you in this book. It is a path of education for anyone. You need not be Buddhist, you need not be religious, you need not even be "spiritual"—in fact, skeptics are most welcome. You do need to be a bit open-minded about the question of what is real and what is unreal. You do need to be willing to learn, to think critically and confidently and question everything. Ultimately you will need to experiment by cultivating both your own good sense and your own inner intuitive experience. After some learning, you will need to meditate and concentrate on examining the mental and physical realities within and without.

Welcome to the path. I hope you are pleasantly surprised by just how real and applicable these teachings can be.

Here we go!

—Robert A. F. "Tenzin" Thurman,
Iron Ox Great Miracle Full Moon, February 27, 2021
*(previously teased in the academy by some students
as "Buddha Bob")*

CHAPTER 1

The Buddha Path

This book is about getting real . . . while having fun along the way. Maybe you're surprised to hear that things like "buddhas," "enlightened persons," "enlightenment," "spirituality," or "wisdom" have anything to do with "reality," and even more astonishing, with "joy" or even "fun." You might think reality is dreadful, joy is all too rare, and fun is childish, while the spiritual life is supposed to be terribly serious!

Let me start right off, since my life has had a lot to do with "Buddhism," which seems highly religious, by saying that what I am going to share with you is not the religion of "Buddhism" but the experience of "buddhasm," the full release into joy that happens when we come face-to-face with the real reality. Our goal here is not to "believe in Buddhism," not to "be religious," not to join a cult or subscribe to a theory. Our goal is to gain the clarity of mindful awareness and the joy of real freedom—no matter what our religion, belief system, or cultural membership. I call that deep experience a "buddhasm." And yes, I purposefully associate it with an orgasm, the blissful transport that every animal approaches with fear and trembling yet craves as a peak experience of life.

Of course, everyone makes a fuss about finding "happiness" or "joy," but few make a virtue out of "fun." "Enlightenment" smacks of 17th- and 18th-century intellectuals like Descartes and Voltaire and the serious business of facing the universe, dismembering nature with "scientific analysis." To be clear, what I mean with this term *enlightenment* includes that too, but more importantly is the blissful fun of life with wisdom and love; it is an extraordinary state of awareness, which we will all definitely get to amazingly soon.

Serious Science

"Science" stinks of chloroform, labs, and people in white coats mixing noxious chemicals, telling us we need surgery or radiation, making bombs, building computers that lock us into information overload and end up with AI-spewing, humanity-despising robots like the Terminator or the Cylons.

Buddha was a scientist, for sure.

Some fun-loving moderns might think that the historical Buddha did show promise as a fun-loving young prince. His name was Siddhartha Gautama and he had a royal throne, a glamorous harem, eventually a loving wife, and then a beautiful son. But then he seemed to go awry: he ran away, starved and tortured himself, and ended up a beggar. But actually, when the young prince gave up the pleasures of family life, he found the far greater pleasure of being a buddha. The great discovery of his enlightenment, the one that made him the most famous Asian person in world history—thank goodness—was that *reality itself is bliss*. In his very first message, offering us the famous four noble truths, he assured us that his third noble truth, nirvana, bliss, that term I used before—enlightenment—is the only real reality of life and death. He stuck to that message ever more explicitly through to the end of his 45-year teaching career.

The Buddha knew that he couldn't immediately announce that reality really is bliss, but have you noticed the grin on the Buddha's face? Have you ever checked it out, Buddha's smile? Big grin. He's very cheerful; Buddha is very happy. When you become a buddha, you have a weird experience first, where you seem to disappear, and everything else seems to disappear, simultaneously. Then the disappearance disappears, and then everything is back. This is the act of waking up and coming to know bliss.

Even better, to fully know that bliss is to *be* that bliss. Such enlightenment is the bliss of experiencing yourself as actually made of light, effortlessly sharable with others. Such enlightenment occurs when you are completely aware of the reality of the world around you, good and bad, while the blissful awakening supports your seeing all the gold and silver linings. You can thus connect soothingly to the tough side of life without getting overwhelmed by it.

A true scientist, the Buddha was totally realistic. That's why, at the moment of enlightenment, he broke out in a huge grin. He realized deathless bliss and expanded his being to identify with everyone and everything, everywhere and everywhen, while purposefully remaining present to others as seeming to be his good old self sitting there grinning under the bodhi tree. Deathless bliss is "nirvana," total freedom from suffering, the blowing away of pain, the profound immersion in the "really real." It is totally good, the ultimately enjoyable experience, the blissful freedom from suffering of any kind, the timeless and timely freedom from death in infinite life.

Sounds good, right? The great fun of it is that you do not need to abandon all your many loved ones; you engage in your world joyously. When you wake up in this way, you effectively help everyone you encounter come to enjoy the very same bliss, which you see they already have deep within themselves. All beings possess this same ability to wake up and become enlightened. What a great discovery!

So, What Is Buddhism, Anyway?

Today in the modern world, Buddhism, as represented by its best leaders, such as H. H. the Dalai Lama, is not a religion seeking to convert you; it is not asking you to drop your birth religion or your secularism. Rather, it offers you a time-tested method of developing your own intelligent understanding of reality, ridding yourself of living in denial on any level. For example, we usually live with the denial of death—you don't think about it, you are afraid it will depress you, so you have no motivation to look into it and you don't want to face it. You think to yourself, *We'll all be zipped up in a body bag, and then will be reduced to ashes*, or something like that. We do allow mourning, but we nevertheless keep up the denial of death, especially our own, whenever upcoming, but inevitable death.

If you live in denial of reality, you will invest your life energy in fruitless occupations. You will want to live in a multimillion-dollar mansion, but all its rooms and views will mean nothing once you die. You still pursue it because of your denial of death. This is an impermanent reality; it is a changeable entity. But if you open up to death, do meditate on it: "This body of mine, this identity of mine as inhabiting my coarse body, I won't keep them. What I do now—maintain house, food, youth, beauty, pleasure—all will be fruitless in the long run."

Of course, you should keep your health to be able to use your mind and body to good effect. But your main effort should be "What am I, where am I, what should I do here and now?" You will focus on how to remain conscious when going beyond your death—on the quality of your continuation. When you do not live in denial of death but wake up, think about it, and meditate upon it, you will be preparing for a good continuation while becoming more conscious about your day-to-day living. You will therefore live more realistically.

If you are a Westerner, or anyone really, and you don't know much about Buddha and want to get educated, start reading some Buddhist texts. You can keep going to your current religion or to your MIT temple of secularism to maintain your belonging to the supportive community you grew up in, but try to expand your education by using the Buddhist literatures and therapeutic practices to become more realistic and have more fun.

You can do yoga to learn about your body, where the cramps and blockages are in your muscles, your circulatory system. You can do mindfulness meditation to learn how emotions arise from ingrained ideas and rote thinking, giving you more freedom and more critical leverage over what you believe and think, and how you react in situations. All of this takes you in the direction of greater realism. And there are many people out there who will try to help you learn more, all without imposing "Buddhism" as a religion.

Okay, okay! Be surprised and skeptical. No matter. I challenge you to take a look at this completely new perspective. Just like the Buddha, *yes, you too* can be a scientist, test these teachings, and ultimately master life in unbreakable joy and overcome all difficulties, if you dare take up the challenge. You too can know freedom from suffering through awakening to enlightenment.

This "enlightenment" I am talking about is totally rational, practical, in solid touch with reality. It is rightly called "realistic." At the same time, it is playfully endarkening, ecstatically transcending, sensually and emotionally fulfilling—as I said earlier, even "orgasmic!"

What I say should seem surprising—even "too good to be true." Hard to imagine, to be sure, but when you can endure even a bit of cognitive dissonance, you can open up a new horizon of possibility. Once you glimpse the possibility of enlightenment, you'll recognize that it was always there all around and within you, but you just didn't pay attention to it. Too good to be true? The good has to be false and the true has to be bad? Who says so? On what basis? See, we are already becoming scientists.

"Buddha-fun" means *you can have it all, you, yourself,* human, American, Hindu, Taoist, Jew, Christian, Muslim, secular humanist, Buddhist, red, black, white (pink, really), brown, yellow, blue, green, Terran, You Individual Citizen of Planetary Society, you there! You are already a "relatively enlightened" person just by virtue of being human. When you dare to know your own real biology at all levels of the material and the mental and the spiritual and the cosmic, this becomes crystal clear. You *can* develop full confidence in your own enlightenment, if you're willing to educate yourself in this teaching! This book can be your golden key to open the door to buddhasm-based science and technology, which will enable you to inhabit your own experience more fully, the really fun experiences you already have yet only fleetingly enjoyed!

Okay—so if I'm already enlightened, why do I suffer so much? We have pain in life because we don't realistically know the truth that we *are* enlightened. Here's the shocker: being in touch with true reality is so powerful that it completely overwhelms any pain, any loss, even of limb or life.

Emptiness and Freedom

In talks I give around the world, I am beginning to refer to this reality more as "freedom" than "emptiness." Why? Emptiness, or *shunyata* in Sanskrit, is an absolute negation, "absolute" in the sense that it only negates and does not imply anything else. "Emptiness" means that all relative things are empty of any nonrelative core or essence. Indian scientists discovered the decimal system, and *shunya* was the word they chose for zero. It derives from a verb root *shvi*, which means "to swell," as a seed swollen by moisture opens, creating an empty space within itself, a void, a free space. But we think of "free" as something good and positive, whereas "emptiness" or "voidness" is intimidating, as it seems so close to nothingness. So "freedom" is a word to watch here, as an encouraging synonym of the famous and still useful "emptiness" that we will explore later on.

Wakeful Consciousness Embracing Cognitive Dissonance

One way for us to move toward freedom is to examine the lens through which we view the world. I think here about the famous "duck-rabbit" Ludwig Wittgenstein was fond of playing with. It is drawn here.

You can see this as an outline of a duck head facing to your left, or an outline of a rabbit head facing to your right. Once you see both, you can snap your recognition faculty back and forth. You can keep your focus and snap back and forth faster and faster until you can almost see both at the same time. Or can you? Are you seeing it one way and then imagining it really fast the other way? What does it take to feel convinced you see both simultaneously? Or does that not seem possible? How many times do you have to flip it back and forth before you see both at once? Or is it like seeing your face in a mirror, where you see a 3D face as if through a window but simultaneously know it is a mirror reflection on the flat, shiny surface? Are you seeing it wrong but knowing it right? Or are you seeing it right and knowing it's wrong? What's the difference? Is there any?

To take things a little further, take note of how you experience this kind of duality/nonduality right in your daily life! How? Just think about the fact that you experience it every night when you fall asleep. At the moment you fall asleep, you let go of awareness and happily slip into unconsciousness—right? If a sense of nothingness existed as your base reality, you would fall into it, since you totally let go, don't you? But then something strange happens—you wake up! And if you sleep deeply with no vivid dreaming, it seems that you have spent no time at all in the unconscious state of deep sleep! Right? Some mornings, if you are still tired from exerting yourself too much over many previous days, you are frustrated that you haven't slept long enough and aren't really rested. So, you have no sense of time when you are unconscious, as well as no sense of space. But you were somewhere, and time did pass, which you know by inference: *I must have been in my body in my bed during the last hours, because here I am again, and it's a fact that some time has gone by!*

Furthermore—and this is really important—you can reasonably think, *I feel better than when I fell asleep, so that spaceless, timeless, unconscious condition could not have been a foretaste of nothingness, which is nothing to be tasted, since it is permanently not there. In fact, there must have been a field of energy around and within me, which has energized me this morning! Wow! I must have been floating in a medium of nourishment! It must be very subtle and easygoing, since it didn't wake me up. And it is always there when I fall asleep and get refreshed, whenever that happens. So it must be there right now, without intruding upon my waking awareness!*

In this way you can begin to strengthen your trust in reality, begin to sense the nature of the freedom of the space-like emptiness. It's different from nothingness. To continue our work as scientists, we can examine these points of cognitive dissonance and see that reality is perhaps a bit different from how we normally perceive it.

Reality Is Fun, I Promise

I feel confident saying that we have all had real fun at some time in our lives. If we are carrying a lot of pain, however, we may not remember having had fun. Maybe it was only in the womb, or at the breast, or maybe in only the tiniest relief in the midst of anxiety or agony, only in the slightest distraction from our pain. If we never had any relief of pain, or the fun of even a tiny pleasure, then why on earth would we be able to imagine it as possible, or why would we lament its lack or absence? When we do have any kind of "fun"—a bit of relief, a moment of pleasure, a consoling happiness, a wave of joy, and even some type of bliss—we still don't think it's fun if we focus on how much more we could be having or if we reminisce about how much more fun we had before.

I aim to show you how you can come to understand that *reality is fun—the playful joy of your life when you're in touch with your own deepest reality.* That understanding will enable you to feel it through and through, in your mind and in your flesh and in your bones. It will lead you step-by-step to discover what the Buddha discovered—that there *is* an ultimate reality, a reliable reality, a durable reality, a diamond-like reality, indestructible. Engaging in that reality is fun, even *super-fun*, and you can find it yourself. You can know it, can feel it, can be it. And the neat thing is that you can be confident you will find it, because you are it, you are in it, as it, already. In fact, there is no other way to reach your super-fun buddha-nature as something else: you have to see-it-know-it-feel-it-be-it as you, yourself, must have always been, in reality.

This is a shock to imagine, of course. If it's too much, you can just dismiss it, since you are free. This is a free life. Whether or not your country happens to be free, the world is free, because freedom is another name for reality: reality is the always accessible face of fun.

Viktor Frankl, an Austrian psychiatrist who survived incarceration in a Nazi death camp, wrote, ". . . happiness cannot be pursued; it must ensue." When you let everything go and fully face the reality before you, even in a condition of profound misery, happiness can well up seemingly from nowhere.

You might feel I have claimed a lot for this book. Some of you might even feel it's like a "pop-out book," and on a special page something will "pop out" and you'll suddenly see, know, feel, and BE ALL THAT YOU CAN BE because you joined something amazing! And off you'll go, like being on a roller coaster, or like a surfer on a big wave!

Well, yes and no! Yes, in the sense that at any moment you could have an epiphany, what in the Zen tradition might be called a *satori*, a flash of enlightenment. The earth could move under your feet, the sky get bluer over your head, the sun burst through the clouds, and the deep connectedness to reality in the center of your heart flash into your awareness. But no in a practical sense, because what we all need is a process of education, or in the case of most of us, a *reeducation*, a *higher education*, even a *super-education*—since many of us have been over-indoctrinated into a worldview that assures us (falsely) that there is no such thing as an ultimate reality that is the free bliss of the sheer joy of endless fun!

The not-just-further, not-just-higher, but *super*-education in this book has three parts: 1) a super-education in science; 2) a super-education in ethics; and 3) a super-education in the meditatively concentrated mind-power that takes the science and the ethics to the summit, to the max.

The Super-Educations in Detail

The three "super-educations" serve as your path to such a state. Though I talk of "path," remember that you are already there, as you will ultimately recognize, so your journey is to find out where you already are. This three-fold path is conveniently divided into eight branches, so it is commonly known as the "eightfold path" of Buddhism, or as I call it, engaged realism. The three super-educations are divided into eight branches of the educational path, each distinguishable from the other and yet all going in the same direction.

The science super-education is divided into

1. Realistic worldview

2. Realistic motivation

The ethics super-education is divided into

3. Realistic speech

4. Realistic evolutionary action

5. Realistic livelihood

6. Realistic creative effort

The mental super-education is divided into

7. Realistic mindful awareness

8. Realistic meditative concentration

In sum, you need to develop your knowledge, your self-control, health, and energy, your lucid wakefulness, and your super-focus. Then you will become able to know what, where, and how you are going to have more fun, while bringing more fun to all your beloved companions and friends and even your enemies (who won't harm you anymore once they are having too much fun to bother).

Now you may be thinking, *Is he talking to me? Why should I do this? How can I do this? Is there some other way for me?* If you're thinking something like that, it's a good sign. Of course, you can find other keys to the door I am opening for you. If you have another key that works for you, more power to you! I do know that this particular set of keys I present in this book works very well; they have been tried and true over thousands of years for countless individuals in numerous languages, countries, and cultures. If you have them in your hand, you might as well try them out. If you change your mind later on, you can always get another set. After all, you are free, you are human, you are intelligent, you are sensitive, and you can make your own decisions.

It may be that the countless beings who have preceded you and me and are now already enjoying the super-fun of enlightenment are monitoring our classroom, this world, and have tweaked our destiny as humans on this planet through our sciences, arts, technologies, histories, and so on. They are following their "Star Trek prime directive" by not interfering openly in our evolutionary progress, but subtly planting hints and clues, as in a gigantic game of *Clue* or *Quest* or *Treasure Hunt*. For example, how about all our different artists, our musicians, our Ravi Shankar veena players with their ragas, our Vivaldis, Bachs, and Beethovens, our Leonardos, Tsongkhapas, Dōgens, Nāgārjunas, our Descartes, Kants, Heisenbergs, and Einsteins, our Shakespeares, Scorseses, Spielbergs, Lucases, our great poets, Sapphos, Kālidāsas, Shāntidevas, Keats, Shelleys, and Emily Dickinsons? They play their instruments, invent their theories, build their mechanisms, tell their stories, write their poems, and sweep us down the rivers in their harmonies and transporting flights of sound and light and vision.

Things seem so desperate today—technologies of environmental pollution, reckless resource extraction, and war-power destruction being so overwhelming as to jeopardize our lives and the future prospects for all beings. It seems as if we have no alternative but to take responsibility for ourselves and do whatever we can to make things better, starting with cultivating our own adaptability and resilience. We also might as well have some fun in the process, as we may have noticed that we are more resilient and adaptable when we are having some sort of fun. Now is the time for all good people to come to the aid of themselves and their world, including their own nation and their neighbors'.

I myself am still a "work in progress," but in the last 60 years, thanks to the kindness of my teachers, partner, children, and friends, I have discovered enough about my own buddha-nature to be confident about yours and to know this book can be helpful.

How helpful? You will end up happier and also a better person. You may well worry that perhaps some can be happy and yet become worse people, being happy in spite of being egotistical and selfish, and even sometimes harming others. But this is precisely where we are wrongly educated and need the Buddha's super-education. Actually, a happy person is not just someone who shouts out how happy they are. A really happy person is one who feels real streamings of bliss and satisfaction in their body and mind, automatically wants to share that with others, automatically feels it unnecessary for others to be so miserable, and naturally has the skillful gesture that lifts others around them into relative good cheer, even just by their presence.

This guidance has come down to me through the ages. I know the spiritual and scientific ancestors in some detail, how they benefited and enjoyed and had fun themselves, and I am having more and more fun myself as I go along. So why should I not give it out from my heart to yours, since the capacity is all already there in each of you? Take it or leave it, it's up to you. Whatever you decide, I wish you all the best of luck and blessings.

CHAPTER 2

The Realistic Worldview

When Buddha felt the bliss of the experience of the full understanding of reality, he immediately saw what had been wrong with him up to that moment. He knew it was the same thing that is wrong with most other people. So he decided, after waiting for the invitation from the powers that be—the "God" of the day, Great Brahmā and company—that he would share his prescription and his therapeutic curriculum. He had previously meditated with a group of five ascetics and so, after a 49-day holiday, he went to see them, his former companions, to give them his prescription for mental and physical health, which he called the "four noble truths."

He called them "noble" truths because these things are true for someone who has achieved a degree of openness and sensitivity that enables them to empathize with others and feel a kind of *noblesse oblige*, a friendly responsiveness to their needs. And they are not true for the ordinary self-enclosed, self-defensive, uptight, self-centered sort of person—everyone who has not gone through some kind of opening experience. Generally, I would sadly say that since then, over the last few thousand years, we're most of us still stuck there at some point. So that's why he called them "noble truths." We think someone is noble when they are the best kind of friend, and these four truths are states of reality, facts of life, not just propositions.

These four truths or friendly facts are still today a model for a good doctor's diagnosis: 1) the recognition of the symptom; 2) the diagnosis of its cause; 3) the prognosis that gives us the likelihood and the nature of the cure; and 4) the therapeutic method that counters the malignant effects of the cause.

Let's break out these four a bit further:

1. The recognition of the symptoms. The symptom that plagues our unexamined and unenlightened life is our constant suffering: the suffering of change as our pleasures fade; the suffering of our pains, such as birth, aging, sickness, and death; and the cosmic suffering of us thinking we are separate from the alien universe around us.

2. The diagnosis. The cause of such constant suffering is our misknowing—knowing mistakenly—that we are really real in ourselves and really separate from the world around us, which leads to the craving and the dread engendered by the hopeless struggle of our small "I" against the huge everyone and everything "other than me."

3. The prognosis. Fortunately, the prognosis is excellent, as deeper examination leads to nondual wisdom. At the deepest level, when we fully realize that in fact "the self" is utterly and harmoniously interrelated to everything "other," we experience the blissful relief of total freedom from any kind of suffering.

4. The therapeutic method. Since it takes effort and time to transcend the superficial stress to reach the deep bliss of the really real, the effective therapy is an eight-lane highway on which to drive the great vehicle of the comprehensive super-education of our whole humanity, transforming and empowering our body, our speech, and our mind to discover who and what we really are.

The Highway with Eight Lanes

The eight lanes of this highway usually have been referred to in English as the lanes of *"right* view," *"right* motivation," *"right* speech," *"right* evolutionary action," *"right* livelihood," *"right* effort," *"right* mindfulness," and *"right* concentration." Translating the Sanskrit *samyak* as the "right" in "right view" reflects the idea of the early English translators that Buddhism must be a "religion" and the lanes of its highway must be a set of religious rules or commandments, against which one's actions can be measured as "right" and "wrong." That is what they expected of a "religion"—that it should have a creed, a set of beliefs and rules of thought and behavior as prescribed by a deity or prophet, like their own Western religions. But the Buddha was not founding a new religion: he was rebelling against the Vedist religion of his culture, rejecting its inadequacy for guiding a fulfilling human life. Instead of enforcing a religion, he was instituting a new system of liberating education.

Instead of saying "right," I use the term *realistic* for the Sanskrit *samyak* attached to each of the eight lanes, since *realistic* is better for *according with reality,* rather than *"right,"* which is appropriate for following a rule, right or wrong. And reality is where the highway leads; it is what we have to work with. (Of course, in matters of practicality, being realistic is "right" and being unrealistic is "wrong," so it's not that far off!)

You may also have heard that "Buddhism" is basically, or even "only," "meditation." And that meditation is the most important thing you can do. And "learning" is okay, but not so important. "Practice," we are told, "is meditation. And that's it! The rest is window dressing." This is misleading, both wrong and unrealistic.

The Buddha makes this clear by placing the realistic view (*samyakdrshti*) as the very first lane of the eightfold highway. Why isn't meditation first? Where is meditation? Well, one kind of meditation is the eighth branch, "realistic concentration" (*samyaksamādhi*), and maybe another type is an aspect of the seventh branch, "realistic remembering" or "mindfulness" (*samyaksmrti*).

When I was just getting started on this highway or path, in my own early understanding, I wanted only to meditate. While reading Nāgārjuna's book, the Tibetan language shone off the page in letters of gold, and I wanted to leap toward freedom from habitual reality. Subliminally, I think I may have wanted freedom from life. I would get so filled with this feeling of nirvana presence, freedom from my worries, freedom from all anxieties and fears, that I would go into a kind of trance-like meditation, and I would actually begin to experience leaving my body, feeling as if I was on the threshold of melting into nirvana as I imagined it. Geshe Wangyal-lah, my beloved root teacher, went to some trouble to actually stop me from meditating. I couldn't believe it at the time since I thought that meditation was the way out of my predicament in the world. He was definitely clairvoyant, since whenever I jumped into meditation, and especially when I began to leave the plane of the anxious mind in the restless body and soar into contemplative spaces of release and ease, he would show up, bang on my door, interrupt me, distract me, and take me back to the path of learning and thinking. Although I would be polite, I would think, *Oh, I can get back to nirvana later. It's there.* And a couple of times I almost did. But my meditation obsession was so frustrated.

Much later, after learning more and using meditation more carefully, I overcame my frustration and realized that this was a great blessing, a deep teaching. There is no use in meditating much until you have learned something and become clear—especially about the way you deeply and unconsciously exaggerate your sense of self. Before you disrupt that habit, heightened meditative prowess will just give more power and armor to that deep-seated self-identity habit. This habit is the seemingly natural feeling of being an absolute, fixed, solid, undeniably present, really real self. The mind is so powerful, if you meditate too much without learning to somewhat neutralize that habit, you can get stuck in some sort of dissociative state.

The Buddha's great discovery came from his sustained investigation of the status of his sense of absolute, intrinsic self-identity, which he spent six years looking for within himself. Eventually, he experienced that sense as baseless, its assumed object, his intrinsic identity, dissolving under analysis; a little scary at first but then immensely releasing. The hard part of his liberating discovery was his experience of his habitual self seeming to disappear into a yawning nothingness, and the amazingly gracious and blissful part was the realization that his relational, resilient, living self was infinitely, blissfully, triumphantly, and responsibly better off without being trapped and subjugated by a false sense of domination by a seemingly fixed and tyrannical self-identity.

His revolutionary discovery gave birth to the first of the eight lanes of the highway, the *realistic worldview*. It is just exactly this deep, visceral, relational, intuitive awareness of freedom, a responsive freedom that automatically expands awareness of every detail of the field of cause and effect within which one is free to make the most realistic choices. This realistic worldview is what Buddhist science most importantly brings to the West and serves as the basis of any useful meditation. Thus the realistic worldview initially has to do with learning, science, intellect, and wisdom and ultimately deploys meditation to permeate all one's emotional and even instinctual being. Once such a worldview becomes clear, then meditation becomes realistic. In fact, meditation at that point is totally necessary to deepen our understanding and open us up to the miracles of relativity, thereby empowering our compassionate activity.

That is why Buddha insisted that the first lane on the highway invites our learning and understanding, and that learning means *understanding relationships*. Not only relationships in the sense of life partners, or parents or children, but relationships within the realities of all that is. This is really the main mantra of Buddha's teaching, its epitome (try not to worry about it being in Sanskrit; it's a powerful mantra):

OṀ—YE DHARMĀḤ HETUPRABHAVĀḤ /
HETŪN TEṢHĀM TATHĀGATA HI AVADAT /
TEṢHĀM CHA YO NIRODHO EVAṀ VĀDĪ /
MAHĀSHRAMANĪYE SVĀHĀ /

OM—Of all things created from causes,
The Realized Lord declared their causes
And their cessation; just this he proclaimed—
All hail to Him, the Great Transcender!

Thus the realistic worldview is the rational acceptance of causation and its transcendence, not blind faith in some authority or guru. It is not even any compulsory belief in the Buddhist "three jewel refuges": the Buddha as the example and teacher, the Dharma as the teachings and the reality taught, and the Sangha as a community of fellow students. It's not even blind faith in nirvanic freedom. Cause and effect are eminently plain to see, which reasonably leads to the Buddhist understanding that there is no single, mysterious cause for things, but rather numerous *causal conditions*, which yet allow transcendent freedom. This is all a part of the realistic worldview that we can test and, if it meshes with our experience, adopt.

The first step toward a realistic worldview is one taken to accept the reality of causation. Understanding cause and effect as both relative and temporally infinite, ultimately beginningless and endless, we then can confront the causal world more creatively, knowing we are both part of it and potentially all of it. We can face its immensity and dedicate our potential infinite energy toward making the world ever better for everyone. Thus facing and embracing the timeless infinity of interdependent causation gives us the strength in every finite-seeming time to learn to cope with reality cheerfully. We can voluntarily engage with it out of an amazing combination of freedom determined by wisdom and necessity met blissfully with compassion.

I'll explain further what I mean by causation here. I am a New Yorker, and once I had an epiphany in the subway that left a lasting impression. I had been practicing and thinking about the Buddhist biological teaching about the beginninglessness of life: that since no something can come out of nothing, all somethings come from other somethings, which solves the chicken and egg problem of which came first. Chickens and eggs just keep on coming, one before the other, back and back until they're lost to view from our point in time. It seems correct, but there was this uneasy feeling about it, as if there must be some place where everything first came from—an original chicken or egg. On the other hand, who says so? Why can't it always have been going on? What's the harm in that? Once you let go of that worry, the implication of beginninglessness for me and you is that we have always existed in some form, having somehow become human in this life. But when I think about it all, given an infinite past with infinite past lives, I cannot rule out already having been every kind of being any number of times. And not only me, but every living being must also be the same. And so, every single being there in that subway car must have been involved with me over numerous previous lifetimes, in every conceivable relationship. No particular relationship can be ruled out in the context of an infinite past of countless relationships.

As this kind of thinking was going through my mind, I kept on glancing furtively at the other people up and down the car, on the East Side Lexington Avenue line, going uptown from Union Square. In New York subways one doesn't stare at other people much. Everyone is busy doing something—reading books, looking at their phones, or staring at the ads above the seats. Suddenly people began to look "familiar." Then it hit me that we had been involved with each other numerous times over numerous lifetimes, maybe as friends, maybe as enemies, maybe as parents and children, maybe as lovers, maybe as sisters or brothers. I had to control myself not to stare at people as they all began to seem so déjà vu!

From this experience, I developed a fantasy to explain to my friends the root of a buddha's compassion, how a vow to save all beings from suffering, a kind of messianic determination, called a "bodhisattva vow," might make sense. If one never meets other beings but once and eventually all beings die and disappear, and then we escape from involvement with each other, there is no need to make such a fuss. But if everyone has been involved with each other beginninglessly, and if everyone is going to continue to be involved again and again, endlessly, it makes sense that our involvement should be optimized. Who wants to fight and hate again and again? Who wants to hurt and be hurt again and again? Obviously everyone should somehow come to love everyone else and each want every other one of them to be happy, if only to prevent their unhappiness from spilling over upon oneself. Everyone should somehow come to help everyone else. So, wakening to this realistic possibility, I can now do my part by promising to optimize my and others' benefit from my side, at least for starters. This is a very realistic worldview that inspires wakefulness and compassion.

How to Actually Develop the Realistic Worldview

There is no better instruction for developing the Buddhist worldview than a short set of verses given by Tsongkhapa, inspired by the angel of wisdom, Mañjushri, and written in a letter to a student of his in Eastern Tibet:

> *Though you may experience transcendence,*
> *And feel the spirit of enlightenment,*
> *Without the wisdom realizing freedom*
> *You cannot cut the root of cyclic life—*

The wisdom of the realistic view is the most important of the three "principles" of the path to enlightenment, the first being the transcendent attitude that lowers the priority of worldly ambitions and focuses on the great quest of life, and the second the spirit of enlightenment of the bodhisattva, the loving will to bring all other beings with you into freedom from suffering; from the first mention of freedom from suffering it is equated with relativity:

> *Who sees the sure causality of things,*
> *Of both cyclic life and liberation,*
> *And ends all objectivity-convictions,*
> *Thus finds the path that pleases buddhas.*

The first step of realism is the acceptance of causation, which implies not continuing to project intrinsic reality, a thing-in-itselfness, into relative things we perceive.

> *Visions inevitably relative*
> *And emptiness free from all assertions—*
> *As long as these are understood apart,*
> *The Buddha's intention is not yet known.*

Here he cautions against dualism, which leads to thinking of the ultimate emptiness and nirvana as a place apart from the relative world of apparent things.

> *But when they coincide not alternating,*
> *Just seeing inexorable relativity*
> *Secures your knowing free of objectivity-habits—*
> *And investigation of the realistic view is complete.*

So when you see things, even in a misperceiving way where they seem like absolutes, things in themselves, the mere fact of seeing them proves their relativity and frees you from being stuck with them as absolutely and objectively separate from you and your experience.

> *More, as seeing clears out absolutism*
> *And emptying clears away nihilism,*
> *You will see freedom dawn as cause and effect—*
> *And will not be robbed by extremist views.*

This final verse is unique in this kind of instruction, as it reverses your meditation on emptiness as antidote for projecting absolute intrinsic identities into self and things, and on relativity as antidote for thinking empty things are nothing, and carries your realistic insight into your daily experience, so your daily life becomes non-dually unified with your contemplative investigation of reality. Seeing things becomes antidote to absolutism and knowing becomes antidote to nihilism. It's what I call the Chinese-finger-trap version of living meditation: it turns ordinary experience into an automatic cultivation of liberating wisdom; pulling away holds you tighter.

This shows that the super-education is not at all any sort of indoctrination, but really a liberation, a path for you to discover your existential freedom in the world. Your commitment to relativity, to causation, becomes the

solvent that erodes your conscious or subliminal entrapment in all the various absolutes supposedly apart from
your immersion in relational life. Our reifying (making a
thing out of a concept) habit is so powerful, we can even
think of a nothing as if it were a something. On the other
hand—this is subtle but important—getting the absoluteness of relativity does not mean resigning oneself to the
samsaric relativity of endless suffering, because viscerally knowing the absoluteness of the relativity seals the
free-flowing bliss that allows your compassion for others'
suffering to overwhelm it.

Thus the realistic worldview puts us on a path of gradual erosion of the fetters that are based in our distorted
inner sense that what we really are is some sort of fixated,
isolated, absolute self problematically and temporarily
enclosed in a relative and vulnerable body, dealing with
potentially dangerous other relative beings and things, all
of which are potentially troublesome for our intrinsically
separate self. Once we keep our focus on our immersion in
causal processes and examine all possible absolutes outside
of relativity, we discover their emptiness of any separate
existence, our own sense of isolated existence dissolves,
and we realize the absoluteness of our participation in relativity, which we can call the nonduality of absolute and
relative. This is the discovery of the relative as the absolute
by melting the projected absoluteness out of particular relatives—this is how wisdom becomes love.

My favorite expression for this is Nāgārjuna's famous
shūnyatā-karuṇā-garbhaṁ, "emptiness as the womb of compassion," or you could call it "freedom the womb of love."
As the Dalai Lama says about the benefit of the realistic
view of nondual freedom/relativity, "Through this understanding of interconnected reality, you come to realize that
if good things happen to others, you will also benefit, if

not immediately, then eventually. If they suffer, you eventually suffer. Therefore, you are better able to empathize with people from very different backgrounds. Compassion for them becomes easier."

Buddhism Is Realism, Not Religion as Defined Today

All of this is to say that Buddhism isn't so much a religion as a worldview. In conversation with His Holiness the Dalai Lama, he and I worked out a fun formula that Buddhism, while highly spiritual, is only maximally one-sixth a "religion," since "religion" is currently defined as a system of ultimate beliefs and associated ritual and moral behaviors; while Buddhism in practice consists of the three super-educations in ethics, mind, and wisdom. Ethics is based on the reality of interpersonal action—in other words, helping and not harming others. Mind is developing stronger powers of self-awareness and self-transforming concentration. Finally, wisdom is the understanding of reality. The confidence in the possibility of understanding the world—that one could become enlightened if one succeeds in the education as to how to control negative habits of body, speech, and mind; broaden awareness and sharpen insight; and explore the nature of reality—is only a provisional belief, seeking confirmation or disconfirmation by your own experience.

Buddhism as a religion is wonderful for some but will not by itself get one to the evolutionary summit of nirvana or buddhahood, which is humanity's optimal condition. However, Buddha's threefold super-education in life, mind, and science will get one to a deeper personal sanity and an appropriate public civility and adaptability on planet earth, no matter what one's religious home.

Way back, before I went back to graduate school, Geshe Wangyal told me I should focus on language, linguistics, and science, and that my work in the future would have to do with Buddhist science. Later, after I received my doctorate, he and the Dalai Lama commissioned me to translate the Tibetan collection of the Buddhist science texts preserved from the lost great Indian Buddhist universities, a collection known as the Tengyur (literally Tibetan for "scientific treatise in translation"). These texts are a 1,500-year codification of the wisdom knowledge that can govern our behavior and interaction with our surrounding animate and inanimate relativities and can liberate us from our mental and physical suffering.

As the original founder of the Buddhist inner science tradition that transformed Tibet, Buddha was compelled by his awakening to reality to serve humanity as an educator, not as a religious prophet, because he knew that you cannot be liberated through blind faith, but only through experiential knowledge—wisdom. Education is the process that brings that deep wisdom forth (*leads* it forth, as in the Latin *educere*) from within your human intelligence and your sensitive heart.

To emphasize, the religious belief component cannot liberate you from suffering, because only wisdom can liberate you from suffering. As the great 8th-century Indian philosopher and sage Shāntideva says in his *Entering the Way of the Enlightening Hero*, "Everything the Buddha taught was for the sake of wisdom." Everything boils down to salvation coming from your own sharp intelligence and your own experiential knowledge, your own wisdom.

Again, as my final slogan, and after 60 years of working with it, "Buddhism" just seems to be realism. "Buddhism Is Realism!" That's my motto! No need to worry about religion, for or against. Just be realistic. It's just the "A," the alpha principle! Nowadays I just want to shout it from the rooftops! Of course, to get the impact of that, you have to know that Buddha discovered that the "reality" you're being realistic about is the bliss you're looking for!

Buddha was overjoyed to discover that the real reality is bliss, the bliss energy of perfect freedom. Therefore the experiential knowledge of that reality is also bliss—body and soul. One merges with it; one melts into the bliss that is release from suffering. One can even say reality is only thoroughly known by bliss, subjectivity itself melted into bliss. Thoroughly knowing it is being it. Ignorance, our misknowing of reality, is not bliss; it is self-entrapment in separation, a state of alienation that faces all the seemingly insoluble problems. Misknowing, misperception, misunderstanding—these cause suffering. They *are* suffering. Luckily, misknowing is never total, as knowing is always coming through in the inadvertent, intuitive, and all-too-often unnoticed sparkles around the edges.

Buddha's discovery of reality was his experience of nirvana: pure freedom. On that happy morning when he fully awoke from misknowing and fully expanded his being through blissful knowing as infinite inter-being, he exclaimed, "Deep, peace, clear light, non-proliferating, uncreated—I have found the one reality, like the deathless elixir!"

When we know true reality, we know total bliss.

Wisdom Is Bliss—Ignorance Not So Much

Luckily, to experience reality as suffering is just a mistake, born of our wrong knowing, the opposite of the realistic worldview. Such deluded experience is not real reality. It is an unreal reality. It is illusory. Reality is bliss-freedom-indivisible. Free of the illusion of alienated self, you know with mind and body that you have always been sheer freedom, which you have either suffered or enjoyed as a wholly relational, loving, selfless self. When you fully experience the nature of the world, no longer separating yourself from "all the other"—i.e., the not-you world around you—you find real bliss, and you never again really suffer. So the "buddhasmic" experience is true realism.

Since Buddhism is realism, the Buddha's enlightenment discovery is that of the true nature of reality and thus is a scientific discovery. It is not a mystical, "otherworldly" experience, though it is "out of this world" great. It is the full experience of this real world.

Here we need to talk a bit more about the physical discoveries Buddha made that are the source of his teachings. Buddha made the most extreme effort to penetrate to an experimental (i.e., experiential) insight into the deepest, most ultimate, "absolute," if you will, nature of physical reality. He put his life on the line to do so—that is to say, he faced death and kept his cool, kept his realistic awareness. He thereby discovered what he called "the clear light of the void": the peaceful, inexhaustibly vibrant yet quiescent energy-plenum of emptiness, or voidness, which is not really a "foundational" or underlying reality. Rather, it is the very actuality of reality, the matrix of all the differentiated things, each and all relationally present, because void, empty, free of any nonrelative component or essence.

In other words, he fully, experientially, realized the nature of this reality with a nondual, immersive consciousness. In a scientific sense, he was clear that it is inexpressible in words and cannot be captured by any positive final theory. It is the nondual absolute, inexpressibly but utterly inseparable from the relative reality we normally associate with.

What I mean by relative reality is that an unknow-
ing, suffering being is one who experiences her-, him-, or
itself as a separate limited entity surrounded by infinite
other beings, things, and energies constantly threatening
to overwhelm her, him, or it. Luckily, such an intolerable
world is only illusory. An awakened buddha being, accurately seeing through the illusion and coming to know
the reality, is fully overjoyed by it. She or he or she-he
experiences her-, him-, or themself as blissfully and invul-
nerably indivisible from the infinite whole of all beings
and things and energies. From such an omnipresent, mul-
tifarious vantage point—from all directions at once, so to
speak—such a buddha being can effortlessly shape her-,
him-, or themself to fit with what all those beings need
to perceive in order to open doors for those beings' own
deeper enlightening experience. This is an inconceivable,
wide-open worldview from which universal empathy and
compassion become totally natural.

From the very beginning, Buddha taught this reality
that he had discovered quite simply as the third noble
truth of freedom from suffering: "nirvana." He allowed
people to understand it in whatever way was appropriate
for them at particular moments in their development. To
some, he allowed them for the time being to think of it
dualistically, as referring to a place outside the world that
they could reach by overcoming their egocentric ignorance and its attendants, lust and hate. To others, he more
precisely presented it nondualistically, as the reality of the
here and now.

He acknowledged right away that it is inconceivable
and inexpressible, so it cannot be embraced effectively
merely as a dogma. Instead, the good news is that you can
verify and experience such reality yourself. That is just
what the Buddha did. He engaged intensively in scientific

exploration of the world, including within himself. When he finally experienced reality to the fullest, he exclaimed, "Wow! It all is blissful, uncreated, and absolutely free, and has been so always. I am it, and all of you are too!"

With that discovery, he knew that all of us can understand it too. He said, "Don't just 'believe' me, or believe *in* me without any reason. You must explore it all for yourself, critique your misknowing ignorance, be sharp-minded, doubt, and investigate. Doubt what I say! Think it over deeply. You must seek it, and you also can discover the deepest reality yourself through a process of total education. Though you at first see it as inconceivable, you can bit by bit imagine it, you will get more and more used to its possibility, and its taste will lighten up your experience of the illusory, which will cheer you up."

Just so, this is the founding of a tradition of joyful scientific discovery, without a doubt. The process of education derived from it is based on the confidence that every human being can discover the very same thing for him- or herself.

The Yak-Tail Flywhisk Teacher

I love the wonderful Ch'an/Zen story from *The Blue Cliff Record* (Thomas and J. C. Cleary translation). It is a story of the meeting of Pai Chang and his teacher, Master Ma, which Pai Chang told to his newly arrived, soon-to-be chief disciple, Huang Po. Ch'an masters used a yak-tail flywhisk as an authority symbol. They would give a flywhisk to graduating disciples as a symbol of their having developed some level of understanding. As Pai Chang told the story to Huang Po: "Master Ma asked me to pick up the flywhisk and then asked me, 'Do you identify with this? Or do you not identify with it?' I answered by putting it back down. Master Ma then picked it up himself, and then I asked him the same question. He made a lion's roar, a shout so loud that I couldn't hear anything for three days!"

As he listened to this, completely open and empathizing with the event, Huang Po was so impressed that his jaw dropped, and his tongue hung down out of his mouth in awe. Pai Chang took note of Huang Po's deep attunement and said, "Now that you have heard the great insight and seen the great function of Master Ma, don't you want to be my successor?" Huang Po right away said "No!" continuing, "I cannot just succeed to you. He who only equals his teacher's knowledge diminishes his teacher's virtue by half. Only he who transcends his teacher is worthy to carry on the tradition." The commentator on the text says here that "to see how father and son behave in that house is to truly understand."

Here you can see how true Ch'an and Zen maintain the inner heart of the progressive Buddhist science tradition—and this Ch'an example, of course, was in the context of the very patriarchal and authoritarian Chinese culture. Confucianism emphasizes the relationships of father/son, husband/wife, etc.—and patriarchal authority is huge, as it was in India in Buddha's time.

Luckily, nowadays, sometimes the good teacher is the servant of the student. The key is to practice this concept when exploring new territory or going over something again. Be the student, with a beginner's mind, no matter how versed you may be in something. There is always something more to understand, and it is the students who bring fresh insight from their lives. Such insight, the essence of genius, brings new knowledge to the teacher, who then becomes greater in the teaching of subsequent students. That is liberal education, the discussion at the roundtable, liberating, not indoctrinating. Learning is not just the regurgitation of some fixed understanding but consists of fresh discoveries that converge in a more realistic worldview. After the student reads what is assigned, you have an open discussion at a roundtable about the subject. It's the idea of equal intelligences meeting, all are learning. In my own history, I have learned more in my role of teacher, many times more than as an official student, from seeing things again and again in the light of the students looking at things afresh.

I'm quite happy about adolescent rebelliousness, though it can be rough on us parents, because it encourages the young to break through and improve upon the stuck qualities of the old. The United States is such a fit place for it, since it can break through the conservative idea that each generation will be worse than the previous one, that we should preserve the old ways and traditions, that the young won't live up to the current generation.

Buddha himself rebelled; he left the palace he was raised in and the Brahmin priests behind. He said to his father, the king, "No! I will break away from all that; I can understand things myself; I can awaken and become enlightened. Then I can truly serve my people and make the world better, not worse." This fits with the American "can-do, can-understand, can-innovate!" kind of thinking, which, though sometimes co-opted by imperialist types, enables breakthrough after breakthrough.

Having left his palace life behind for that of a scientist, Buddha explored reality as it is and made many discoveries, cardinal among them being the reality of selflessness or emptiness. All things accepted in his day—such as the Great God Brahmā and the various impersonal "transcendent" absolutes—he found wanting, in the sense that they all are empty of any absoluteness, self-subsistent essence, intrinsic reality, objectivity, or identity. They all disappear under analysis that probes them to the core and finds no thing there. Indeed, their emptiness itself, the freedom from fixed identity, is actually their only intrinsic reality, and that emptiness itself is also empty of its own intrinsic reality. Thus every thing is only relative, free of any absoluteness.

The Buddha shared the teachings on emptiness to free us from our habitual entrapment in supposed absolutes, thus showing us how to develop a realistic worldview. As the great Indian poet Matrcheta wrote in the 3rd century CE:

Buddhas do not bless away others' pain with hands,
Nor do they wash away their sins with cleansing waters,
They don't transmit their realization into others' minds—
They free them by showing them their own reality!

The main point is that the realistic worldview melts all absolutisms into emptiness. Once you realize emptiness, you are compelled to learn to surf the causalities of the relative world around you toward both your own realization of the wisdom of nirvana and your compassionate purpose to include others within it. This happens naturally because the realization automatically opens you to identifying with all others, and so your own realization does not separate you from them, and so must include them. The bliss of nirvana eternally includes everyone and everything, and so you find you are all reality, melting into this infinite, eternal space-time-reality-identity through total, inexhaustible, immutable bliss that automatically enfolds all others as well.

Another way to think of the realistic worldview is that you're here forever, and you have to be concerned not just with your old age and your pension but with your next life and the ones thereafter. The way to be concerned for your next life is to invest now in your higher mind and get your mind open and clear. Practice and meditate on generosity. Give something to somebody, a little bit, especially something you like. That's the best kind of offering: that which you already like, you give away.

Don't overdo it. Don't push so far past your habits that every time you see that other person with that thing you gave, you regret, "Oh, why did I give them that thing?" Don't overdo it. Baby steps, baby steps. Little by little, bit by bit. Share your *mousse au chocolat*. Don't take the last three bites. Have the first three bites, and then just give. Don't give the whole thing away and then watch with annoyance as the other person enjoys it; enjoy it a bit yourself and then enjoy them enjoying it.

Once you have that realistic worldview, and you realize you are a precious continuum of good energy still dragging along some bad energy behind you, your job as a human is to take this unique opportunity to really increase the good exponentially and really decrease the bad exponentially.

One example of someone who was able to adopt the realistic worldview and exponentially increase the good was my teacher. My beloved Geshe Wangyal-lah led me into the heart of the Tibetan language—itself a divine, magical creation—and gave me the keys to this emptiness-relativity tolerance equation. A simple, unassuming man, he preferred to tend the flowers in his garden in the gentle hills near the Delaware, shunning a highly merited acclaim in the forums of philosophy in Tibet, India, or America. But he was the most profound philosophical genius I have encountered—from the little bit I was able to recognize. He exemplifies for me the central fact that heartfelt philosophy is no mere word game, but is the ground of a life of purpose, transformation, sheer joy—tolerance in little things and selfless effort in the bigger ones. His daytime garden was lush and beautiful in his later days, with roses and peonies and bright orange tiger lilies, and he was never happier than when he carefully watered them in the cool of the late afternoon. But for me his most wonderful garden is ever, to borrow the Tibetan Buddhist master Tsongkhapa's exquisite metaphor, the "night-lily garden of the treatises of Nāgārjuna," in other words, the divine song of the awakened mind that comes as a result of a realistic worldview.

CHAPTER 3

Realistic Motivation

Once your worldview is realistic—once you accept the evolutionary causality of mind and thus are aware of both the danger of letting it go in the wrong direction toward greater forms of suffering and the opportunity to make it go in the right way toward greater happiness and bliss for self and other—then you are motivated to find the shortest, quickest way to the best, the unexcelled supreme good. Your realistic motivation, simply put, is to become fully awake.

When I was younger, I remember feeling alienated from my family, friends, and schoolmates. I knew I had a special purpose but no one could help me find out what it was. Others tried to impose what they thought it should be, according to what they thought I was and who I should be. I felt like a stranger in a strange land, to quote the title of Robert Heinlein's well-known sci-fi book.

As Ganden, my perceptive eldest son, whose blessed purpose of this life ever goes mysteriously beyond mine, eventually said, "Somehow, wherever we are, we are always wandering in exile!" Maybe it is because I was born and raised in New York City, Manhattan, itself an island in sort of a concrete exile from the earth—except for the blessed Central Park. Both of my parents were nominal, non-churchgoing, for the most part, Protestant Christians. My father had a soft spot for St. Francis but did not go to church. My mother's Bible was the collected works of Shakespeare. I personally never had much love for the God concept—probably from the very time I was born, according to my mother.

When I was ordained as a Buddhist monk and eventually returned from India and visited my mother in New York, coming from my local monastic home in New Jersey, she said to me, "I should have realized you would become a Buddhist. When you were a baby and I took you to our Brick Church to be baptized, you were so disturbed and upset that you kicked wildly in your long white gown and knocked over the baptismal font and drenched the priest. He was so embarrassed that he just wrung a few drops out from his cassock on your flailing feet and counted that as your baptism! You were resisting the church from the beginning!"

A few years ago at one of the Dalai Lama's talks, when he said he didn't want people to convert from their birth religion to Buddhism (as a religion), I reassured him from my seat next to his translator that I had not converted from Christianity to Buddhism but instead had added being a sort of a Buddhist to being a reason-yogi seeker. In fact, Buddhist science ultimately taught me to take more interest in Christianity, as well as in all other long-serving religions. Thanks to His Holiness, I now really love Jesus and Mary, Confucius, the Shekhinah and Moses, Radha and Krishna, and Shankara of the nondualist version of Hinduism, Laozi and Taoism of course, and Islam, starting with the great Muhammad, Kadijah, Ayesha, and then especially his Sufi successors like Attar, Ibn Arabi, and the amazing Rabi'ah of Basra. I can even get along with G-d! (I love that the Jewish sages gave G-d a name—YHWH—without vowels so it cannot be pronounced, being on guard against their own arrogance of trying to control things by calling out their names.)

When I first read the Buddhist teacher Nāgārjuna's deep explanation of Shakyamuni Buddha's four noble truths, they hit me viscerally. Each noble truth—or as I like to say, friendly fact—was completely on target. I immediately realized that these four noble truths were my exact prescription for a cure, a fitting conclusion of my pilgrim-seeker's journey to the East that ended up via India in New Jersey, just an hour or two west of Manhattan!

The purpose of a human life, it became clear, is to attain that perfect freedom, that *summum bonum* (Latin for the "highest good"). Imagine what a bad situation it is when a culture imprisons its members' aspirations by instilling in them a sense that there is no such thing as a summit of good—just survival from meal to toilet to meal, waking to sleeping to dreaming to waking, from birth to death, and finally to nothing! The Indo-Tibetan Buddhist science and civilization opened the door for me to a life purpose that suited my instinct that there is such a supreme good, and that compared to it no lesser life goal is worthwhile.

The very highest good becomes defined within infinite space and time as perfect awakening and enlightenment—being buddha—being blissful happiness overflowing outward as love and compassion and art that enfolds all the living in the golden light of abundant fulfillment and joy. It is the summit of the individual's evolutionary struggle, the loving drive to become a being of perfect freedom, perfect bliss, perfect wisdom, and perfect love, and the power to make it so for everyone else, past, present, and future, as well as for oneself.

As ever, the main revelation of the four friendly facts or noble truths is the third—the end of suffering—which is the prognosis for healing our illness of misknowing. There is a real nirvana, a blowing away, and such a free-bliss nirvana is and has always been the actual reality of our life and death. When we fully understand it all, we will know and experience life as bliss, realizing that our previous suffering was only in error, not totally unreal but ultimately illusory. This nirvanic reality is still portrayed unrealistically by some dualistic Buddhist traditions as being a state outside of, elsewhere from, the world—a real state apart from the seemingly equally real world of suffering. In fact, that notion of a "radically other" nirvana is simply the irrational mistaking of a relative state for an absolute state: it is merely a projection from the misknowing sense of having an absolute self that is independent from everything else!

If nirvana is somewhere else, it cannot be an absolute state, it cannot be reality. It's just another place, right? And if there's a state of being in nirvana that's separate from your being here, then it's relative, and so unreliable or changeable.

So Buddha, when he was being very logical, said to an audience that could kind of take it: "Nirvana is reality itself, and always has been. And therefore, you don't actually enter it; you discover that you've always been in it." It's what you discover.

In my own early learning days, I was certain that nirvana did exist as a place; it was a real turn-on for me, this possible freedom from suffering. But I also felt, mistakenly, that nirvana was located elsewhere—that it was a space outside, that the world was mere illusion, and that the idea was to get out of it and into the trouble-free nirvana that seemed to be out there waiting for me. This dualistic way was how I understood nirvana in relation to samsara—a term that refers to the karmic evolution–driven endless cycle of life, death, and reincarnation.

I knew immediately yet inexplicably that there was such a thing as nirvana, such a freedom—perhaps this strong feeling came from a previous life! It was as if I always expected it and did not doubt it at all. But I did think of it as being elsewhere, as somewhere else to go; because I had a strong sense of feeling separate from everything, I wanted that separateness to be confirmed forever.

I easily accepted the first noble truth, the pain of all the struggling of the seemingly solid, independent self versus the universe. Once there seems to be a real separation of self from the universe, then others seem really to be "other" and we enter into conflict with them. It is when we lose that struggle that we experience the truth of suffering.

The second noble truth I also understood right away as pointing to the negation of the illusory sense of separate self, but yet still wanting that separate self to become a selfless nirvana of a final apartness from the world around me.

I was still selling short the third noble truth, however, the one that's really true as a depiction of reality—Buddha's great truth, his great discovery. I so wanted it to be a final separation, a state beyond. By calling it a final nondual state, I was able to ignore the fact that its imagined apartness was the final hideout of duality: the duality between the relative world and an imagined non-relational reality located outside of it and apart from it, yet accessible to me.

This self-centric psychosis about nirvana does not get beyond the first and second noble truths. As long as one misknows reality, feels separate from others, and reifies the self as the real thing, thinking that others are very different, then birth, life, death, and relationships are all unsatisfactory; they cause suffering.

The dualistic understanding of a nirvana apart from the world around me—the way I understood nirvana at first—fit with my immature, escapist feeling that I wanted to reach a pure space away from everything. I thought one had to leave the world to find peace and satisfaction, so I misunderstood the real meaning of nirvana. Still, I was very gung ho. But Geshe Wangyal saw this escapism in me—just as the Buddha saw that tendency when he was teaching egoistic, mostly male Brahmins and saw their escapism, their seeking after someplace to get away from it all to a road less traveled, or perhaps a road of no more travel! The fact that the goal of nirvana can be misperceived as a realm apart makes it a less effective path of a seeker's evolution, because it leads to an addiction to quietistic states of aloofness, dwelling happily in contemplative realms wherein one cannot easily develop one's compassion for others.

Compassion is the most important aspect of full enlightenment, because without it one too easily enters a state of being unmoved emotionally. By the way, there are people who achieve awakening without compassion. They do become a kind of saint, because they are beyond crude drives that lead them to cause harm to others, but since they see through others too easily, their motivation to love them and help them free themselves becomes weak. They tend to rely on full buddhas (those who become awake and nurture compassion) to do the job rather than feeling the intense motivation to become buddhas themselves, to take responsibility for others.

The fourth noble truth, the path, seemed sensible to me. I didn't like that the eighth branch was meditation, or samadhi—i.e., one-pointed concentration—and that the first branch was a realistic worldview. I wanted meditation right away. I was impatient to get out of the world—I was tired of ideas and I wanted to get away. I had had enough. Being so impatient meant that starting with the realistic worldview was very difficult for me. I did it, though; I soon relished the first branch, realistic worldview, seeing it as indispensable to the other seven branches—realistic motivation, speech, evolutionary action, livelihood, effort, mindfulness, and samadhi concentration. I loved all eight of them and wanted to fold them all up in the eighth, samadhi meditation.

I was frustrated at that point by my teacher. He skipped passages in Nāgārjuna's book we were reading, those on *dhyāna* ("zen") and *samādhi*, those meditative kinds of things—he skipped the details. I did love that book. And there was a funny thing. When I read it in Tibetan, I felt it viscerally. But in English, after we translated it, I didn't connect to it in quite the same way—maybe, again, that was some memory impression from a former life.

In my first popular book, *Inner Revolution*, I talked about "life, liberty, and the pursuit of *real* happiness" (that's the subtitle), since I was fitting nirvana in with Thomas Jefferson's "life, liberty, and the pursuit of happiness." People focus on the first noble truth, the truth of suffering—even Buddhist teachers, since it fits with the miserableness of people. It's amazing how people feel anxious but safe being

miserable! After all, what we call happiness is usually ille-
gal! When you feel really happy, you feel frightened, or
at least nervous. We are indoctrinated to think this is a
dangerous letting down of our boundaries. It's too intense,
like an orgasm—it's too high and it will lead to a downfall
that will come afterward. People look at you dubiously if
you're too happy.

Just imagine this: you're a parent, and your kid comes
home and says to you, "I'm so happy! The world is so beautiful! Everything is wonderful!" Are you happy? No. You
immediately ask your child, "What happened to you? Are
you on drugs? Are you drunk?!" You freak out! You have
difficulty accepting that they can be happy for no reason,
that they can have this inner feeling welling up from their
heart, that they feel happy, truly, and you can't believe
that there are no dangerous side effects.

If you do manage to accept it in someone else, you
feel left out—subconsciously or consciously, you are jeal-
ous. You think, *What about me? Why aren't I happy too?*
The truth, the announcement by Buddha under a tree,
is that the actual reality of the world is, itself, freedom
from suffering—he is saying that it is bliss already. He
doesn't make too much of a fuss about it at first, this cessation of suffering. He tends to cater to the immature,
first level of hope that is kindled in the egocentric person who is sunk in the well of habitual suffering. I don't
mean that moralistically; I'm talking psychologically. I'm
making a structural statement about someone who thinks
his or her center is real. Such a person cannot imagine
one's being in total bliss while still being connected to
all else. Such a person sees relief from suffering as a kind
of dissociation from everything else, just as I did. Fortunately, thanks to the Mahayana, the universal vehicle, to
my teachers, Geshe Wangyal-lah, His Holiness the Dalai

Lama, and later Nena, my wife or "home guru," I eventually overcame this idea that the state of nirvana is outside the world. For some people, though, some of the time, it's not a bad thing that they think that. And certainly, even though the bodhisattva is still in the world for the sake of others, being utterly free of her or his own suffering, it's just like being in another place, a different world entirely! That's why nondualistic Buddhist teaching can support a dualistic approach.

Theravada Buddhism and Absolute Happiness

Theravada Buddhism, the most basic branch of Buddhism that has been around for thousands of years, which I call "individual vehicle" (never the standard "lesser vehicle"), is still relevant and highly valuable today because it leads you to seek a state that is different from what you know. It doesn't matter how you imagine it when you seek it. You can inaccurately imagine nirvana as separate from the world; it still motivates you to find absolute happiness. Absolute happiness and absolute suffering may seem like different things, but they are connected, inasmuch as the motivation to be free from absolute suffering is what leads you to find absolute happiness.

This is why dualistic Buddhism is the base or foundation of nondualistic Buddhism. The ordinary person cannot imagine a state of complete freedom in bliss while remaining aware of interrelationships and being connected. Such nondual reality is rarely possible for a beginner. For example, when I heard the third noble truth—that this presence of reality I first assumed was outside of the relational web was actually within and all around me—my hair stood on end. As a samsara versus nirvana dualist, I still wanted to be free of myself, only happy if elsewhere.

The fundamental predicament of self and other is that when self and other are seen as intrinsically really different, the encounters between them are married to so much painful contact, with so many sharp edges, and they are highly problematic. According to Buddhism, during countless lifetimes we have been killed, eaten, and tortured by other beings, and we have reacted to others by developing internal sicknesses. Understandably, this leads to a deep, instinctual fear of encounter with an "other."

The second noble truth, the cause of pain, is the delusion about the absoluteness of the separateness of self, i.e., the delusion regarding the intrinsic objectivity of the self. This becomes a self-fulfilling prophecy: when one is under this delusion, contact with others does tend to become a bit stressful. If we can make our own body into something separate in our minds, then everything else is suffering. So, at the beginning of my practice, I was trying to get away from the whole thing.

What I didn't know then, and had never heard of, was that the negative result of that kind of mistaken view is found in the teachings as "attaining the cessation of sensation and conception at the wrong time." I had never heard of this and didn't know what it was about. But from my present vantage, I can now understand the great kindness of Geshe-lah, my teacher, and his incredible skill, because I think I had a kind of dualistic experience of the nirvana-threshold states, which are called the four formless or immaterial trances (some translators use the word *absorptions*, which makes me think of Bounty paper towel ads).

Anyway, I was so into the development toward this realistic motivation—full liberation—I felt I just had to become a *bhikshu*, or Buddhist mendicant monk. I wanted to have no other concern in life, in principle, than learning, meditating, and realizing the nature of reality, which is the complete liberation from suffering. One of the problems was that again, my teacher Geshe-lah refused to make me a monk. He said it was fine for me to live like one, as I was doing, and focus as much as I could on the positive development purpose. But in the long run, it would not be my lot to remain a monk: you have to stay for life in the Tibetan tradition or it is a shameful embarrassment. You can't be a monk for a while and then quit. He acknowledged that I was sincere and had no such intention of quitting and truly wanted to be a permanent monk. He just knew from his experience, his knowledge of my past lives' momentum, perhaps, that I would not be able to remain a monk. I had a different destiny. Regardless, I disobeyed my teacher and bugged him about being a monk. I wanted more meditation and a more formal way of being a monk. He admired my resolve but insisted I be more practical and listen to his advice. I could not do that; I was too stubbornly insistent on my view and plan. Though I kept learning a lot, we were at this impasse.

Later I found out that there are some circumstances wherein one has to stay a layperson and develop the other-engaging, self-giving virtues as well as the self-improvement ones. The very key is to create a new form of super-education, to create a big change in our society and radiate it out from America throughout the world. Not through military regime change and so forth, but through art: the art of happiness, of joy, the art of mindfulness, yoga, and meditation. In this magnificent enterprise, India, its civilization and complete culture as restored by the Tibetans bringing back India's own long-lost Buddhism, is our key ally, along with all the indigenous earth-centric cultures of the planet.

Buddhism without Buddhism

Buddhism is not only entering the West via traditional Western Buddhist publications such as *Lion's Roar, Tricycle*, and so forth; it's also coming in via *Scientific American*, for example. Mindfulness has gone mainstream. I gave a series of lectures in California in the 1990s entitled "Buddhism without Buddhism," in which I said that Buddhism would be countercultural at first—first viewed as an artifact of Buddhist countries, that it naturally started that way—but that it would go mainstream when people saw the importance of mindfulness, self-cultivation, and self-applied mental hygiene and put it into their lives without becoming "Buddhists." Then it would become an innovation in our own culture, and people would use it happily, and it would deliver real benefits.

Think, for example, of Jon Kabat-Zinn's work on mindfulness-based stress reduction (MBSR) and that sort of thing. People are bringing Buddhism into a more mainstream role via education, and they're even getting away from the term *meditation*, for example, which is perceived as countercultural by some, seeming a bit like a heresy. Instead, they're going with phrases such as "mental hygiene," or "concentration," or "anti-ADHD therapy"— that's how it is done. You can be a member of another religion and still engage in these practices. To make Buddhism more mainstream in the United States, you can do what His Holiness the Dalai Lama does with utmost sincerity: insist that the main thing is to understand—there is no need to "convert." It's preferable to remain with your family religion, or nonreligion, but you can still listen to lectures on Buddhism and experiment with "Buddhist" practices simply as educational experiments for the mind.

The procedure of teaching and learning that Buddha put forth in the eightfold path is preserved in all forms of Buddhism whether or not they are explicitly so labeled. This being the case, Geshe-lah's interrupting of my unlearned, escapist, meditation-trance efforts and his insistence that my life-purpose would not be accomplished by my being a monk, as admirable and necessary as that was in general, turned out ultimately to be a real godsend. This is a very important point to make to new Buddhists, old Buddhists, and modern Buddhists, who tend to think the doorway to Buddhism is meditation and asceticism. Some even say that Buddhism itself is *only* meditation, only withdrawing from the world, which is very wrong.

Buddha taught the dualistic form of Buddhism to his less emotionally developed disciples, mostly highly intellectual, world-weary male Brahmin ascetics from the priest class with a very strong sense of self-absolutization, who wouldn't have been able to easily imagine the world of life and death, pain, women, kitchen, cooking, hunger, injustice, etc., as nirvana, no matter their level of sophistication. And that is what I wanted to do right away: jump into a trance—a seemingly uncompounded transcendental state—and consider it a done deal, apart from the lousy world.

Where Buddha left the door open for them (and me) was that he never clearly described nirvana as such an absolutely abstract state. On the contrary, he did clearly describe the quite attainable four absolute-seeming bodiless, formless trance states of infinite space, infinite awareness, unconscious nothingness, and beyond consciousness and unconsciousness—and he clearly stated that none of them is nirvana!

The realistic worldview and therefore the realistic motivation (or life-purpose) are the first two branches

51

of the noble eightfold path. Realistic worldview is where you have to learn and critically reflect with your thinking power to develop wisdom. And once you develop critical wisdom, even on a discursive level, then your intention or life-purpose to travel the path to enlightenment as the meaning of all of your lives, the present one and all your future ones, becomes the inevitable, logical step from your realistic worldview. Why waste your precious human lifetime doing anything less than using every conscious moment to evolve toward buddhahood?

If it is one's life-purpose as a human evolutionary being to attain the bliss of enlightenment, and you feel much better when you adopt this super-motive, then you also must develop the altruistic mind of love and compassion for all beings to bring them with you, to share your bliss with them. That spirit—the spirit of universal enlightenment that makes you a bodhisattva, or open or awake-hearted being—is the cause of the firm stability of buddhahood, the blissful way of remaining in the world for the benefit of others while always feeling the blissful presence of nirvana permeating the entire situation.

Once realistic worldview and realistic motivation for self and other are in place, the ethical branches of the path automatically follow—one lives with realistic speech, action, livelihood, and creative effort, and on that calm and loving basis, the mental branches of realistic mindfulness and concentration become possible and fruitful.

Now, if we have come to understand our life-purpose as using the amazing human life-form we have achieved to evolve toward its summit perfection of perfect wisdom and perfect love and compassion, we embark on the ethical transformation that is required. It is interesting that this begins with realistic speech.

CHAPTER 4

Realistic Speech

The first two branches of the eightfold path, realistic worldview and realistic motivation, constitute the higher education in wisdom. This is the scientific exploration of reality as we experience it, and we transform our experience by understanding it.

To activate the third branch of the path, we move from the super-education in wisdom to the super-education in ethics, which requires us to learn more about how ethics connects to evolution. First of all, we have to acknowledge the evolutionary power of speech, words, and language in order to use them to reshape our lives along with others.

The three path branches constituting the super-education in ethics are:

1. Realistic speech
2. Realistic evolutionary action
3. Realistic livelihood

Why begin with realistic speech? Because good evolutionary actions begin with learning. The realization that actions are evolutionary in their causal impact on oneself and others mandates one's choice of livelihood.

Ultimately all eight branches of the path must function simultaneously. Their order of presentation emphasizes a best sequence of approach, but they are not rungs on a ladder, where you step off one to get onto another. They are rather like a symphony—you add one instrument at a time until all are playing harmoniously together, and each one comes into its fullest power only when combined with all the others.

Scientists, Politicians, Artists, and Educators

In many discourses, the Buddha describes realistic speech as speaking the truth and avoiding falsehoods; speaking diplomatically, reconciling others' disagreements and refraining from divisive speech, slander, and backbiting; speaking sweetly and pleasingly, avoiding abusive speech; and speaking meaningfully, avoiding senseless chatter. None of these four types of realistic speech is fanatical, since one should not use truth to cause harm in certain situations, should not be diplomatic unless it will help the others involved, should not flatter people who are in error or misbehaving just to please them, and should at least withhold meaningful speech in a situation where you know someone will misunderstand. As in all things, pragmatism is essential.

Speaking truth is what scientists are dedicated to doing; they investigate reality and must try to report on what they find, or at least what they consider the truth. Speaking diplomatically is the focus of peacemakers, those who seek to help others improve their relations with each other, serving humanity in that way. Speaking pleasingly is generally good for one's own relations with others, and the sweetest speeches are the creations of artists—poets, playwrights, novelists, musicians, bards, and singers. Speaking meaningfully is best for everyone to do, and especially the responsibility of educators, those who help others become more realistic by sharing reality—Dharma—with them, insofar as they have some deeper experience and knowledge of it to share.

Speech Creating Connection

Speech is the particularly human deep way of interconnecting with the minds of others. When you talk and I listen, I open my mind to yours, letting your thoughts direct my attention. When I talk and you listen, you do the same for me. When we read the recorded speech of people from the past, we share their minds, and when future generations read our thoughts, we share with them. Thus, each of us has the responsibility to be wakeful of what effects we are producing in others' minds when we speak, and when we listen, we also have the opportunity to enter into others' experiences of things we cannot experience ourselves.

Speech should be only truthful, it should be only peacemaking, it should be only gentle, and it should be only meaningful. Babbling meaninglessly, or harshly, or untruthfully, or to make people enemies with each other, those kinds of speech are really negative actions. When you listen to someone, they have the privilege of being in your mind temporarily, and they should not abuse that privilege by talking rot. They should try to help your mind. When you speak, you shouldn't invade other people's minds and speak a bunch of nonsense and rot and lies to them and distress them even more than they've already been distressed. Speech enables us to learn and thereby to evolve, to grow into wiser, more experienced, more realistic, more capable, and happier beings.

Learning new things may even be the essential purpose of all living beings, essential to the quest for true happiness in any one life and along the range of limitless ongoing lives. Human beings, angels, titans, and gods are distinguished by speech. We humans live and evolve in speech, not only physically and mentally in body and mind but spiritually and ethically. Speech has a central role in shaping reality, body being shaped by mind, and mind by speech. Through speech we individual humans can expand our self-identifications to become communal beings without necessarily losing a sense of individual responsibility.

As the great Tsongkhapa said in his enlightenment poem "The Short Essence of Good Eloquence":

> *Of all the buddhas' many deeds*
> *Their deeds of speech are the supreme,*
> *For this very reason, the wise*
> *Applaud the buddhas for their speech.*

Words Shape Our Thoughts

In the most high-tech, advanced, esoteric ways, speech actually controls how we shape our bodies and minds. Speech at its most poetic and powerful becomes mantra when it liberates the mind. Vajradhara Buddha made this famous statement in the *Esoteric Community Tantra*: "You should create your mind with your body-form and your body with your mind-form; and shape your mind's form with your inner formulation of your words."

Following that principle, we use words to shape our thoughts and our thoughts to shape the physical instruments of our experience. It is thus no wonder that the super-education in ethics begins with the cultivation of wakeful, realistic speech.

Speech is of course the place where we transcend isolated individuality and live in community with others, as words are shared between minds and meanings are shared between cultures. To emphasize, when we listen, we open to others' minds; when we speak, we are admitted into others' minds. Speech exists inside us, outside us, in between inside and outside, and beyond all such dualities.

This shared community is not a new condition of Westerners. In the *Noble Teaching of Vimalakīrti Sutra*, when Shāriputra, the ancient Indian saint and foremost individual vehicle disciple of the Buddha, is asked by the Wisdom Goddess to tell her how long he has been in what he thinks is his privately attained nirvana state, he doesn't answer; he keeps silent. She asks him, "Why, Venerable Elder, you are 'foremost of the wise.' Why do you not speak? Now, when it is your turn, you do not answer the question!" Shāriputra says, "Since nirvana is inexpressible, goddess, I do not know what to say!" She then rejects the usefulness of that silence in this case by saying, respectfully but firmly: "Venerable Shāriputra! All the syllables pronounced by the Elder have the nature of nirvana! Why? Nirvana is neither internal nor external, nor can it be apprehended apart from them. Likewise, syllables are neither internal nor external, nor can they be apprehended anywhere else. Therefore, reverend Shāriputra, do not point to nirvana by abandoning speech! Why? The holy nirvana is the equality of all things."

This is why realistic speech, the beginning of the super-education in ethics, is actually the guiding energy of all education in nonduality, which also transcends the duality between the pair, duality and nonduality, not by merely avoiding duality through a dualistic silence.

Speech as Essential to Learning, the Mainspring of Wakeful Ethics

One reason why many Western teachers and practitioners of Buddhism shy away from understanding the three super-educations in ethics, mind, and wisdom that constitute the Dharma in practice, referring to them as "the three trainings," is that we've all been educated a lot already. Many of us have gone through eight years of primary, four of secondary, four of higher, and three to seven of professional education, and yet we're still anxious, insecure, volatile, and often depressed. Our education in Euro-American culture has not solved our problems of suffering! But that is not the fault of education and the speech it depends upon; it is the fault that we have yet to become properly educated to use speech to transform our minds. The educational speech of our materialistic culture is too unrealistic. It discourages us from understanding, persuades us that we cannot understand, indoctrinates us, and traps us in absolutisms and nihilisms. We have to become more self-aware and critically minded, and we will thereby easily see that ours is still a backward culture in some respects. Our worldview puts us in the awkward position of seeking knowledge of a material universe, a frighteningly infinite mass of quantities, the knowing of which involves counting and measuring them, which is obviously an endless effort and therefore a hopeless prospect. We are told that true wisdom is impossible, and so it is presented to us as tantamount to resigning ourselves to our inability to understand what we really are, what life is, and how we should live. So we have no alternative but to fit in with whatever orders we happen to fall under, and this is supposed to be okay, since it all doesn't really matter, it all comes to nothing at the end of the day. No wonder we become depressed, since in our heart of hearts, we sense that it does matter, that everything matters, and that there is more to it than just giving up the quest.

Luckily, there are enlightened beings, buddhas, awakened to reality and blossomed into meaningful abilities to help, whether Buddhist or whatever else. The enlightened speech of such buddhas is realistic; it is scientific speech, which can often verge on the poetic. Aware of its limitations, since reality is ultimately inexpressible, it is also aware of its effectiveness in generating the experience of the inexpressible, which leads to positive transformation, frees us from negative conditioning, and opens our way beyond our assumed limitations. All super-educations rely on speech to direct the mind.

The Core Curriculum of the Enlightenment Buddhaversity

The whole of the Buddhist educational tradition resulting in the great Indian Buddhist universities of Nalanda, Vikramashila, Vallabhi, and many others was based upon the realistic worldview and the realistic life motivation that comes from it. These fall into the realm of philosophy when philosophy is recognized as the original foundation of science. The Indians, Chinese, and Persians knew this and built their civilizations on it, and the Europeans also followed this definition, starting with the Hebrews and the Greeks.

The entire Buddhist tradition is built on a philosophically scientific foundation, which is a way of realistic intellectual understanding, opening out into an experiential encounter with reality at its deepest level. Realism is the key to understanding how education affects one's multi-life evolution. Otherwise, contemplative expertise without realistic understanding could result in one becoming trapped in seemingly divine and highly seductive altered states beyond that of the human, and therefore less apt than a human to achieve the superior freedom of nirvana, wherein nirvana is experienced nondually as the actuality of the world.

Any enlightenment-oriented curriculum, for example that of the new Nalanda University in India, should be based on the three super-educations of the eightfold path. And the upshot is that once liberated in the reality of freedom, one comes to see the beauty of the world, the joy of living as a resilient being compassionately interconnected with all sentient life. Such evolved and enlightened students break free of arbitrary limits to their curiosity and then naturally launch into the specialty sciences known nowadays as physics, biology, psychology, botany, and so forth, and the many arts such as literature, medicine, law, engineering, politics, diplomacy, and computer science. Such genius students will automatically pursue advanced research that is mindful and ethical. Such scientists see ethics as a biological, evolutionary necessity—which is the relevant understanding—and thus are not distracted from their driving motivation to improve the lives of themselves and all others.

An enlightenment-oriented core curriculum should seek to produce ethical persons as a first prerequisite, which involves helping students be *wakeful and lucid in their actions of body, speech, and mind*. It should produce altruistic social actors, determined to make their life's essential purpose the improvement of the lives of others, whether through a profession, politics, business, or the arts. It almost goes without saying that it should awaken an appetite for lifelong learning and sharing their learning through realistic speech with others by educating them skillfully. When the Dalai Lama accepted an honorary degree from Columbia University, he thanked the assembled dignitaries among faculty, trustees, and students, praising the role of education as essential to personal and social well-being. But then he expressed his concern about our curriculum, as he understood it, saying that it was too much focused on producing a clever brain, and not enough on producing a good heart. A clever brain without a good heart, he continued, is unsatisfying to its possessor and perhaps even dangerous to the society. All nodded with smiles and approval, but change has been slow to come.

The Inner Sciences and the Love of Wisdom

Shakyamuni Buddha was the founder of the inner science tradition in our recorded history, and therefore the founding philosopher scientist of the Indian Buddhist inner scientific philosophical tradition. For many centuries, his legacy tradition in India was not called "Buddhism" (*bauddhatā*), but rather "Inner Science" (*adhyātmavidyā*). He first discovered emptiness/relativity and taught the two-reality theory of relative and absolute, or superficial and ultimate realities. He was not a dogmatic religious teacher but rather a dialectical educator (like Socrates), or even a super-psychotherapist, engaging in realistic speech when teaching and thus healing different individuals according to their specific needs. He was also a skilled sociologist and had a deep understanding of the social and cultural currents of his era, and so the teaching and the educational movement he founded were strategically designed to effect changes in society as well as changes in individuals.

Although he was born and educated to be a king of one of the important Indian city-states of the time, we can soundly consider him the initiator of a "cool revolution" designed to gradually change his caste-ridden, warrior- and priest-dominated patriarchal society into the more egalitarian, open, civilized, enlightenment-oriented society it eventually became. He invented a form of mendicant monasticism to counter the warrior militarism of his times and to serve as the nucleus of the educational institutions that gradually sprang up.

During his lifetime he kept his most radical, Centrist philosophical teachings largely esoteric among the advanced students, as the times were not yet ready for them. He predicted that a great mendicant and teacher, with the word *nāga* (a type of mythic water spirit being, part dragon and part serpent, yet able to manifest as human) in his name, would emerge around four centuries later and spread the more radical teaching then, when the culture would be ready to absorb it.

Sure enough, Nāgārjuna (circa 100 BCE–500 CE) showed up, and still today is considered worldwide to be one of the most important world philosophers. Buddhists often call him a "second Buddha," and the profound concept of the emptiness of all things, which he rediscovered as the central focus of the universal vehicle *Transcendent Wisdom Sutras*, totally reshaped the character of Indian and pan-Asian thought and education. His nondual Centrist teachings hugely reinforced the mendicant monastic institutions and enabled them to expand into flourishing universities.

This culture persisted for many centuries, and realistic speech served human needs so well that it spread throughout Asia without any kind of crusade, and individual students came to the universities from all over, as far east as China and as far west as Iran, possibly even Mesopotamia, Egypt, and Greece. The Tibetan empire began sending scholars to the Indian universities from the 7th century, and Tibet gradually reformed its imperial, militaristic, conquest culture into a dedicated vessel of the inner science culture, translating the great books of the Indian university libraries and adopting the inner science curriculum. Therefore, a thousand years ago, when the peacefulness of the Indian nations educated in this way made them vulnerable to invasions by more violent cultures from the north and west, the Tibetans were able to maintain the tradition and refine it further right up to the present day, when it too was violently destroyed by British imperial and Chinese communist colonial invasions in the 20th century. The resilience and power of Tibet, visible in exile still today, come from its thousand-year educational development and cultural transformation that instilled in its people, at home and in exile, a deep dedication to the protection of realistic speech.

Imagine what a culture must be like that loves such a story as that of the crown prince Kunāla, son of the Emperor Ashoka in the 3rd century BCE. Prince Kunāla was famous for his beautiful eyes. His father had a much younger favorite queen for a time, Kunāla being a favorite son by another wife. The new young queen fell in love with him, but out of loyalty to his father, he rejected her advances. A woman spurned, furious, she vowed revenge. Soon she took her chance when he was out leading an army in Kashmir on a campaign to pacify a rebellion. She forged an imperial edict to some generals in the field and sealed it with the emperor's "tooth seal" by slipping the letter into his mouth when he was sleeping; it announced the discovery of a plan by Kunāla to use the army himself to rebel against the emperor and gave orders to punish him for this treason by blinding him. The generals thought it must be a misunderstanding and didn't want to do it, but Kunāla insisted because a "tooth-sealed edict" of the emperor could not be disobeyed. He was blinded with a red-hot poker.

Amid the agony of the first eye being burned out, he remembered in a flash his previous lives, especially the one where he had been a hunter, had trapped a herd of 500 deer in a box canyon, and had blinded them all so they could not jump over the felled trees blocking them in. He remembered having lost his own eyes in hundreds of lifetimes since, as the karmic evolutionary result. He realized that his two beautiful eyes of this life were the last two he had to lose. He attained a deep and complete realization of nirvana during the agony of the second eye being burned out. The generals were amazed to notice that the agony was overridden by his spontaneous bliss of liberation, as his mind found refuge in the super-subtle level of reality free of all suffering.

He also realized spontaneously that the wicked queen had conspired to send the false edict, and he didn't want to go back and cause her to lose her life, so he told the generals to report that he had died in battle. Then he wandered off as a mendicant beggar into the town. Soon a young woman met him, fell in love with him, and became his attendant, and he became well known as a wandering minstrel singer. He had a beautiful voice and people loved him. He did not return to the palace and happily wandered free with his companion, sharing joy as a singer, all blissed out in nirvana.

The Importance of the Teacher

Realistic speech is not just preserved by cultures but by teachers and texts. While reading from Nāgārjuna's *Friendly Letter* with the good Geshe-lah, I must say I felt released by hearing, meditating on, and discovering a bit about the four noble truths or friendly facts. When I heard about the possibility of nirvana being not just the mental but also the physical reality of the world (in Nāgārjuna's nondual vision of the ultimate unity of samsara and nirvana), I actually felt quite exhilarated from the relief of it. I mistakenly thought I had actually attained nirvana for a while, thinking that the oneness of samsara-nirvana meant that the relative world disappears and you are just impersonally present in an ocean of bliss, without a body. I did indeed disappear a few times, and found it very refreshing, like a sound night's sleep.

It was at this time that I first learned the universal vehicle concept of the buddhas' reality. I began my 60-year, still-unsuccessful attempt to encompass fully their nonduality, which until now is only accessed by my educated imagination. But I do take some consolation in the reasoned approach learned from the great Nāgārjuna and his followers, that everything in the "infiniverse," as I prefer to call it, is nothing other than the buddhas' reality body. So even though I feel lost and alienated and frightened of the global apocalypse I see coming, I still feel that all will be well, even after major devastations and individual deaths and rebirths. Or something like that! And it was Geshe Wangyal-lah who first opened that door for me, for which I will forever be grateful. He was a true spiritual friend, which is what the Tibetan term *geshe* really means, the Sanskrit Buddhist notion of the teacher as "the gracious friend" (*kalyānamitra*).

In any enterprise dedicated to learning through realistic speech, the question of finding an appropriate teacher becomes important, since a good teacher can help a lot to intensify learning and development. A not-good teacher would be someone pretending to be more enlightened than they are in order to dominate others, using what is the very worst form of unrealistic speech. It exploits others' desire to evolve toward enlightenment and harms them by misdirecting their life's efforts, often leading them eventually to become disillusioned with the pretending pseudo-teacher, and because of that, despairing of the effectiveness of the teaching itself, and maybe of any teaching whatsoever. The evolutionary consequences of inflicting such harm are said to be extremely serious.

I feel compelled to include a note about finding a true teacher here, as a good teacher can deliver realistic (and thus helpful) speech to a student. Any student bent on the challenging, even apocalyptic, tantric vehicle must visualize the three jewels of Buddha, Dharma, and Sangha as embodied in a living teacher (her or his mind as buddha mind, speech as buddha teaching, and body as buddha emanation). It takes great courage and sincerity to attempt such an imaginative transformation of the human reality of the teacher. The sense of immediate presence of the enlightened ideal is needed because it counters the tendency in historical religions to think that the founder is gone, the age is dark, and so the practitioner can only emulate or hope for great progress in future lives, since enlightenment is something too far away from the present situation.

Actually, the esoteric focus on the teacher merely explicates what is implied in the general universal vehicle nondual teaching: that nirvana is beginninglessly the reality of the world. The buddhas see all beings as completely one with their reality body, that oneness only being obscured for the unenlightened by their misknowing sense of alienation. Thus the performer of the practices eventually realizes that the buddha awareness is already within them, just hidden behind the addictive and objective veils of misknowledge. So, ahead of that time, when they imagine that awareness as being there, as one with the awarenesses of all buddhas, what they are imagining is what is already the case, from the buddha's own enlightened perspective. In this way, imagination serves as the template for realization.

Realistic speech leads us to awakening. It is wrong to think that you can't possibly attain enlightenment because you are so weak and stupid (whereas others are great), and that you can't meet any truly enlightened person. There really are enlightened people—sensitive, compassionate, skillful—who can teach us through the means of realistic speech. I have met a number of them and have been greatly blessed. Of course, I am not absolutely certain how enlightened they really are, since I am not fully enlightened myself yet—so I might be mistaken. But they fit all the definitions I have heard.

An interesting thing that I first read in Lama Rendawa's commentary to Nāgārjuna's *Friendly Letter* is the analysis of the double bind—that you cannot realize selflessness unless you hear about it from another who has realized it, and also, you can only realize selflessness yourself! This means that the limited, self-centered individual can only realize it if he or she hears it from one who has already realized it—and then, he or she can realize it similarly. It's a quadruple bind, actually. So the genuine guru or lama is essential to inspiring and motivating the disciple to fully wake up her- or himself.

I think that Geshe Wangyal certainly realized a great enlightenment, and so has the Dalai Lama, as well as his teachers and some of his colleagues. Due to their kindness, I somewhat understand it too, certainly not fully, but enough to help others begin to get the point and dare to try to find it for themselves. The need for a beneficial lama is really critical, but that doesn't mean a political czar—it's worse if it's some kind of dominating social or political authority. In that sense I prefer to refer to "teachers" as opposed to "masters," though I admit you can say "master carpenter," "master tailor," etc., so you should also be able to say "master teacher."

In Tibetan Buddhism the word *lama* has a different emphasis than the Sanskrit term *guru* does in Vedism and Hinduism. In Sanskrit, guru means "heavy," and in Hinduism there is this "heavyweight" connotation of guru, derived from the cultural weight of the patriarchal father figure, the head of the family. The guru is a heavy weight on your head, a religious authority, a boss-like figure. But a lama should not be heavy; he or she is *bla na med pa* (Sanskrit, *anuttara*)—someone beyond whom you cannot go. You cannot get beyond her or him, because she or he is envisioned as a doorway to omnipresent nirvana and buddhahood. Instead of a boss on top, the lama is like flypaper on which you get stuck—you can't get beyond it. You are automatically opened in the field of such an enlightened, open being, and you become even freer by connecting to the transparency of your own self. So your self-habits can dissolve more easily.

A great example of the subtleties of a teacher and their realistic speech is a scene from the first American Kālachakra initiation in 1981 in Madison, Wisconsin. The Dalai Lama had finished a main part of the initiation, and he put on a certain ceremonial hat, turned gravely toward us all, and said, ceremoniously, "Now I'm your guru, and you have to do what I say." Then he took off the hat, complained about having to wear it, scratched his head, and added, in a completely conversational tone, "Except if what I say is stupid, never mind—just forget about it!" Some of us laughed and enjoyed the relief, but many people were chagrined! They just couldn't bear this abrupt turnabout! They wanted to maintain the spell, the magical feeling of solemn presence, the secure feeling of dependence on authority. But His Holiness was doing the honest thing.

And then there was the example of my first teacher: I can't tell you how many people I saw in New Jersey who came to be his disciples and whom he sent back to independently face their lives. He never kept someone whom he thought he was not helping. Geshe Wangyal passed away in 1983, and until the end I remained connected with him, visited him as a friend. And he did a lot for me. For instance, he asked his students to pray for me so I would get tenure at my college. When I saw them, they would say, "So, do you have tenure now? We're tired of praying for you every morning!" He was my real spiritual father. That's why I say that Khenpo Ngawang Dorjieff, who was his teacher, was my spiritual grandfather. I don't think of myself only as the biological child of my father, gentle descendant of a redneck clan from Mississippi and numerous generals produced at West Point. I also think of myself as a spiritual child of Geshe Wangyal.

Speech is a magnificent thing. That's why they say the greatest thing a buddha does is teach. Because what do we do when we speak? When we have a conversation, when you speak to me, your mind is shared. You share your mind with me when you speak to me. When I speak to you, I share my mind with you. So, in a way, when we listen to each other, we open our mind to the other, give them the privilege of entering our mind by saying something. To treat our speech as such rehabilitates it so that it becomes truly realistic. After this rehabilitation of speech as realistic speech, highlighting the central role of education, we can turn to the evolutionary causality analysis for the conscious evolutionary ethical development of our full body, speech, and mind.

CHAPTER 5

Realistic Ethical
Evolutionary Action

Now we have the distinct pleasure of turning to a break-through insight that reveals the Buddha's achievement as a biological scientist—Shakyamuni Buddha as super-Darwin. I am pleased to stand up scientifically, logically, and philosophically for this transformative understanding, which gradually dawned on me over the decades it took to deepen my appreciation of the Buddha's scientific acumen. As my trust in Buddha has grown—painstakingly, due to my own subliminal embeddedness in materialist culture, my skeptical turn of mind, my conditioning to expect the worst of everyone and everything, my fear of success and real happiness (whenever I have had a whiff of total bliss it has frightened me too)—my enthusiasm for investigation has intensified, my reasoning has sharpened, and I have understood things he taught in new and deeper ways. I can't even believe I didn't see it before; I have come to respect the power of the unconscious blocks to my understanding of reality.

Not so long ago, His Holiness the Dalai Lama wrote a little book on "secular ethics." I knew he was doing it to help the many people, such as "hard" scientists, who are allergic to religion. When I complained to him about his use of "secular" in the title because of its anti-spiritual connotations, he disagreed with me, saying that "secularism in India is respectful of religions!" Conceding that it implies pluralism in India, I still insisted it had anti-religious connotations in the West. Though he held his ground, ultimately he called the book *Beyond Religion*, to my relief. I resisted his using the word on the cover in America, even though it was my most revered teacher's idea.

After some time, it came to me that he was rightly resonating with what the Buddha himself had done in his own era, repeating it in the context of modern thought. The Dalai Lama might not have known that himself, analytically, as in his present life he has not studied the language of the Vedas and their Sanskrit commentaries. Here's the key point: before the Buddha's time, *karma* did not have the present Buddhist meaning he gave it of "the causal, intentionally committed ethical/unethical actions" that give transformative results in the future life destiny and life quality of the actor. In Vedist terms, it meant "action in a ritual," a ritual aiming to placate the Vedic gods. Since it was believed by the Buddha's Vedist contemporaries that the gods controlled beings' fates, action in a sacred ritual that placated them and induced them to provide a good result for the acting person was considered the powerful, destiny-determining action. They called such ritual action *karma* since they thought it determined a person's fate.

But the Buddha, when he realized how life-causality—i.e., biological causality—works more realistically, understood that individuals in the ocean of infinite relativity determine their fate and transform themselves by what they do in ethical or unethical actions—not only bodily actions but also speech actions and mental actions. So instead of the gods controlling your destiny, you control your own destiny by how you act in environments and situations with body, speech, and thoughts in your mind. Because people of that time thought of *karma* as the word for destiny-determining action, he took the word out of that religious context and used it to it refer to "secular" actions that impinge on the world and others around one—ethical or unethical actions that give rise to good or bad results, respectively.

Thus he took the attribution of destiny-determining power away from the gods and their attendant religious priests and their sacred rites and revealed it to be a "secular" matter of an individual's actions in the world. He also was kind enough to come up with a secular ethical description to help his contemporaries improve their actions and their lot in life, just as the Dalai Lama—clearly Shakyamuni's worthy successor—was kind enough to do the same thing for today's scientists and secularists.

Long before Charles Darwin, Buddha observed that humans have a total kinship with other animals, all beings having minds and ever-changing souls (super-subtle-energy-minds), including beings that Darwin would have considered spirits or fairies, and a huge zoology of subhuman beings, as well as deities, angels, and devils. The numerous types of deities have varying degrees of knowledge and power, although Buddha agreed with Darwin that there is no omnipotent One, no supposed absolute "Creator."

Buddha observed this profusion of life more directly than Darwin did, simply by remembering in the moments just preceding his complete enlightenment that he himself in his beginningless past had personally experienced countless lives in every conceivable animated life-form. He was utterly astonished: "I was one of those in such and such a realm, such and such a planet, such and such a species, occasionally human, in such and such a country, such and such a family, with such and such a name, etc., etc., and one of those over there, and one of those others too!" He remembered having been not only human many times, but every other kind of being as well.

Buddha, with his super-subtle micro-consciousness, would also have been aware of the interconnectedness of species through various super-subtle structural codes, which we only recently discovered and now call DNA and RNA. He no doubt welcomes them and other discoveries of recent times (I purposely use the present tense, as I will explain in the context of his buddhaverse, my fun term for the more usual "buddha-land," buddha-field," or "pure land"). But he is more interested in the codes of action by which an individual of any species can shape her or his or its own destiny while transmigrating through various embodiments from life-form to life-form.

The natural reality of the former and future lives of beings fits with the law of the conservation of energy: that no energy is created from nothing and no energy utterly destroyed by "becoming nothing." It merely changes form and can both dissipate and reconnect. The human mind and subtler spirit are some sorts of energies, however subtle. That is the common-sense belief of everyone, really. So why should that subtle mental and super-subtle spiritual energy be the sole exception to the thermodynamic law of the conservation of energy? The body eventually becomes worm food and soil if you inter it in the earth, and heat, smoke particles, and ashes if it is burned in fire, and they themselves become something else. So why should the mind not have its own level of subtle energy continuity—as a natural process, not anything particularly "supernatural"?

As I mentioned before, when I was a recently ordained monk, sitting quietly meditating in the New Jersey monastery chapel with a candle in the middle of the night and actually getting into a nice state, my dear Geshe-lah suddenly came into the room and interrupted me, switching on the overhead light. He asked me what I was doing, and, blinking in the bright light, I said, "What do you mean? I'm meditating, of course! I'm trying to attain enlightenment."

He scoffed, "Oh, don't bother yourself. You can't attain enlightenment—you're an American!"

I was annoyed and said, "What do you mean? I am a Buddhist monk; I totally believe in former and future lives, and I'm certainly going to attain enlightenment. Never mind that I'm an American!"

He persisted, "No, no. It is the mind that attains enlightenment, and Americans don't think they have a mind."

I continued to protest, and he laughed, and having interrupted me, invited me to have some yogurt in the monastery kitchen. I continued to argue with him about this for weeks on end. But then I finally had to recognize that in my unconscious mind, deep down, my education—not spiritual education, but arts and sciences education, if you will, my "material reality" education—had implanted in me a strong certitude that only matter existed, of course convertible into energy. But that no nonmaterial entity, so-called "mind," could possibly exist, could possibly "matter." So I had to admit that Geshe-lah was absolutely correct in the way he challenged me.

Consider that the core misknowledge that causes all pain and suffering is the certain sense an unenlightened individual has of her or his utter separateness from all the "otherness" in the universe. The obvious worst-case examples are the lifetimes spent in the "hells" (*naraka*), horrific zones within which beings unsuccessfully try to ward off the most hostile "otherness." Buddha's biology uses a scale to classify life-forms that runs from the extreme of separateness in hellish shapes and environments to the extreme of inclusiveness known as buddhahood, where one experiences oneself as inseparable from infinite others.

A buddha identifies with all beings and experiences her- or him- or itself as one with all unenlightened beings as well as all other enlightened beings; she-it-he thus does not therefore destroy or abandon anyone in the past, present, or future. It-he-she thence naturally and automatically functions to liberate unenlightened beings from their pains by helping them destroy their own pain-causing delusions, whatever it may take and however long it may take for them to do that—and such help is spontaneously delivered everywhere with maximal efficiency by means of limitless emanation bodies (*nirmānakāya*).

It solves a lot of things, this inconceivable yet dissonantly acknowledgeable idea of a scale of being, from most alienated—marking everything as "other"—to most unified, as is the case in buddhahood. It is a departure from conventional wisdom to realize that Buddha's karma theory is *scientific*, not "religious" or "mystical" or even "spiritual," as if opposed to "material." It's a sophisticated, elegant, biological evolutionary theory accounting for the way in which the lives of beings are shaped. Karma is introduced in all of the Buddha's teachings, especially illustrated in the *Jātaka* tales, the *Legends* (*Avadāna*), the original *"Just-so" Stories* (*Itivṛttaka*), and in the scientific philosophy instructions such as the *Karma Sūtras* and *Abhidharma* texts.

Buddha understood life directly through his own experience. He remembered his own infinite past. He knew that beings need to make sense of their lives in a realistic way in order to thrive, by using their opportunities as human beings in a skillful and fruitful way. He was very clear that theories about relative realities are only relatively true or false and therefore can never be made into absolutist dogmas. Thus, in addition to their practical factuality, their elegance and usefulness are also part of what makes them relatively true in specific contexts. In this way, the Buddha promulgated a theory of evolutionary causality of individuals as well as species that attributed to the subtler energies of the mental and spiritual an important role in the biological evolution of living beings.

Karmic Evolution

Karmic evolution is described as what explains the varieties among forms of beings—why beings are different, why they look different, how they improve and deteriorate; human siblings and even twins look and are different and have different outcomes in life. Buddha explained the biology of this with his theory of individual and communal evolution and his declaration of the causes of causal things, expressed in his cardinal mantra *ye dharmāḥ hetuprabhavāḥ hetūn teṣāṃ tathāgata hi avadat.* Darwin explained this in his own way 2,500 years later by discovering that natural selection via genetic mutations in different environments was responsible for differences in life-forms and the destinies of living species. Watson and Crick came up with the double-helix pattern of molecular genetic coding only a century later, just a few decades ago.

All of these theories give a good basis for explaining the mutations of species on the coarse level of material process, developing a useful biological science. We can easily see, however, that this science cannot connect in any predictable way with fundamental physics at the level of the subtlest particles. So it is the amazing fact that, to this day, only the Buddha and his successors have been able to take account of and figure in the key role of the subtlest energy levels of individual animals' bodies and minds. These Buddhist scientists connected beings' minds and mental actions with the epigenetic shaping of their mutations as individuals. They provided plausible ways of tracking their individual migrations via the death-rebirth process, migrating from embodiment in one species to embodiment in another species, as well as moving from one body to another among a single species' different types and environments. They described their individual evolutions and devolutions during the beginningless and potentially endless involuntary and unceasing quest of individual sensitive beings for freedom from pain and enjoyment of happiness.

In the Buddhist case, an individual is charged with creating a karmic evolutionary trajectory through the causal engagements of body, speech, and mind. The causal process itself—of individual intentional actions having determinative impact on future forms of life and future experiences of the individual—is called *karma*, which simply means "evolutionary causality." In modern terms the causal processes of mutations of species' life-forms over generations is commonly called *evolution*. In both theories, species or individuals can evolve upward toward fitness or flourishing or devolve downward toward extinction or greater suffering.

His Holiness the Dalai Lama complained to me once that karma theory did not pay enough attention to genes and parental heredity. He specifically was comparing the Great Fifth Dalai Lama to himself. In the case of the 17th-century "Great Fifth" Dalai Lama, his parents were yogis, Nyingma school tantric adepts, who had psychic powers and were skilled in magical, supernormal perceptions and actions. But in the case of the 14th Dalai Lama, his parents were farmers, they practiced animal husbandry, and they had no such developed spiritual capacities for him to inherit. His wonderful mother had great compassion, but neither parent had supernormal powers. His Holiness seemed to feel dissatisfied with his genetic heritage in this regard!

In the same way that the 14th Dalai Lama is bringing scientific understanding into conversation with Buddhism, it would be a big shift for scientists to consider karma theory, to overcome their bias against rebirth or reincarnation, and to realize that mind is part of life and is itself a force in nature.

Workings of the Inner Science–Based Biology

Scientists need to acknowledge that whatever their theories of the causalities that shape life may be, they affect how humans think of themselves, what they think their life is and what their life-purpose is, and what they think their best choices are to do with their lives and energies. If individuals do not have a realistic worldview, if they think they are nothings and their lives are meaningless, they will live recklessly and randomly, which will tend to be destructive and will tend to depression. If they realize that every relative thing has cause—is caused by something and serves as cause for something else, even its own deterioration—they will be more careful about what they cause and will use such a viewpoint to analyze with greater care what it is that brought them the effects they experience. I am reminded of the sociologist Michelle Alexander, intrepid author of *The New Jim Crow*, who wrote recently that she wished people did believe in their own future lives, as then they might behave less cruelly and irresponsibly.

Thankfully, one can't say realistically that any individual can become "a nothing"; even in the commonly accepted theory of material energy, there is the thermodynamic law of the conservation of energy. So there is no final end to everything, no landing in a supposed "nothing," just as there is no primal origination of everything from another supposed "nothing." Among all the things, the mind is some sort of entity; it has some sort of energy and its different phenomena have causes, which go backward in time in infinite regression to the beginningless, and which cause something further going forward into the future. The mind continuum becomes an infinite process also, and minds, like bodily forms, arise and decay, and mutate into other forms of mental experience and even into other physical embodiments. There is no such place as "nothing" into which they can go. It is not an empty space, not a location. "Nothing" is precisely the word that lands nowhere, has no referent. There is no there "there." It cannot be a destination.

Such is the most plausible, rational explanation of mind. Mind *is* part of nature, mind *is* part of biological process, it shapes material forms and is shaped by them. It is simplistic and dogmatic to insist that matter is the only thing and mind is just an illusion produced as the brain's epiphenomenon. This is completely irrational. "Minds can make choices to drop bombs, minds can decide to kill or save lives, but they actually don't exist!" This is ridiculous, purely dogmatic, not even sensible, and certainly unscientific.

So we can imagine that the only way to be truly secure is to somehow relax the mind into an open state, called an awakened (*vibuddha*) being, a perfectly evolved (*prabuddha*) being, a buddha, a being that has opened to feel that all reality is its body. And we can further imagine that such a buddha being would be inexhaustible in drawing from the infinity of relativity the energetic creativity to enfold any beings—who experience themselves as stressed or suffering or even extremely tormented—in the very same awareness of their own primal infinite free-flowing bliss that a buddha being timelessly enjoys.

So now, given the scale running from most extreme constriction to infinite expansion, from agony to bliss, our evolutionary purpose seeking secure happiness becomes how to evolve toward the bliss and away from the agony. There are innumerable formulations, of course, but very useful are what are called the tenfold paths of positive and negative karmic evolutionary actions of body, speech, and mind, ranging from coarsest to finest. "Skillful" action is ethical or virtuous action that benefits both self and others, and "unskillful" action is unethical and vicious and harms both self and others.

Skill in virtue becomes skill in evolutionary progress. The ultimate skill, of course, is to go beyond unconscious, instinct-driven evolutionary action and to act only consciously, only wisely, only lovingly, to benefit all beings by introducing them to the reality ocean of nirvanic bliss. The way to get there, though, is to follow the tenfold path of positive evolutionary action and avoid the paths of negative karmic evolutionary action.

Navigating Karmic Evolutionary Action

There is a story that, in a previous life of the Buddha, he received a set of teachings from a great sage who wanted him to value them so much that he demanded the bodhisattva, enlightening hero, use his own skin as a sheet of paper, make a quill pen from one of his own finger bones, and write down the pattern of the tenfold path with his own blood for ink. The sage then recited the negative ten and positive ten together, which the bodhisattva wrote down in the briefest shorthand—he had skin in the game, you could say, so worked for brevity.

To put the unskillful and skillful evolutionary actions together, the three unskillful and skillful bodily actions are:

1. Not taking lives; saving lives.
2. Not taking what is not given; giving everything.
3. Not engaging in harmful sex; engaging in beneficial sex.

The four unskillful and skillful verbal actions are:

1. Not lying; telling the truth.
2. Not speaking divisively; speaking reconcilingly.
3. Not speaking harshly; speaking sweetly.
4. Not babbling pointlessly; speaking meaningfully.

The three unskillful and skillful mental actions are:

1. Not hating; forgiving and loving.
2. Not coveting; being detached and generous.
3. Not being unrealistic; being realistic and wise.

Mental thoughts are actions that have evolutionary consequences. You can kill (hate), steal (covet), abuse sexually (be unrealistic, uncaring) by thought, or save (love), give (be generous), and benefit sexually (be realistic, caring) by thought. This means you must learn to think with love, generosity, and care. Hence your natural focus on being mindful is for your own evolutionary benefit, and luckily, what benefits you inevitably benefits others.

The human form is more expansive than crocodiles and rhinoceroses, with greater variety of thought and behavior. It can expand endlessly through memory and imagination and can also contract dramatically. Killing another living being diminishes the killer's empathetic incorporation of life. The killer thinks he or she drives the victim out of the world and away from her or him forever. But actually, he only cuts the victim's mind's connection to the victim's body. Further, he cuts off his own empathetic connection to the victim's form of life while reinforcing the paranoia that all others want to cut off his, the killer's, life. The victim resents the killer for taking her or his life and carries on into his or her next embodiment an at least subliminal intention to take the killer's life in revenge.

It is said that the Roman Emperor Constantine's wife insisted that the emperor ban the teaching of rebirth in future lives and execute the patriarch Origen, who vigorously taught the law of "metempsychosis," the reincarnation of souls in other bodies, because as empress, she had ordered many executions. She feared some of the executed might take rebirth as a being wishing to take revenge on her, so she wanted the possibility banned, naively thinking that an imperial ban could stop the actual consequences of her actions! Before that, reincarnation or metempsychosis was commonly accepted in Mediterranean cultures.

By contrast, the lifesaver embraces the other's life, identifies with it, expands their own sense of life force by identifying with the other. Saving someone's life is virtually saying, "Your life is connected to mine; I identify with you. I don't want to deprive your mind of its body. My life is greater through your presence: you are present in me, and I would be less without you!"

Similarly, when taking what is not given to me—when stealing—I disregard your ownership, I negate your mind, take your thing from you, discount and disidentify with your sense of self as invested in your possessions, and decrease my identification with your life. When I give to you, I enjoy your ownership of the thing I owned; I enjoy it more through your enjoyment of it. I become greater by enjoying with you more things than I can enjoy just on my own.

When I lovingly merge with you, which I can only do when I offer you the freedom to give yourself lovingly, we become one and, at least subliminally, we experience self-transcendence in communion with one another. We open our very most sensitive hearts and experience freedom as joy, tasting the true safety of reality beyond the fear of harm or death. Sexuality is the place where any animal, and all the more the human mammal, naturally identifies with another, even if it's often only momentary. Your self-giving human nature is mobilized and you experience the melting of boundaries into one another. You expand your sense of identification; you touch the deepest forms of expansion through bliss. Therefore, to use that occasion to be harmful, physically or emotionally, either by rape or social destructiveness, breaking others' relations through adultery, causing social conflict, endangering the other—this disconnects you from expanding your identification with the life of someone with whom otherwise you and he or she can experience tremendous interconnection.

Speech is the form of action where the self interconnects with others by sharing experience through language. Being heard is being given the privilege of temporarily occupying another's mind; listening is opening one's own mind to another.

When you lie and deceive others, you imprison them in an unreality; you excise them from your reality and lose connection. When you reveal whatever you know of truth to others, you expand your world and invite them into it.

When you speak divisively to put others into conflict with one another by slandering and backbiting, you endanger them and sever your connection with them both; even though you may think you get closer to the one, you alienate yourself from the other. When you reconcile them with each other, you share your world wherein they can love each other. Then, actually, they both can feel your friendship and you expand your world by being accepted into their worlds.

When you abuse the privilege of being heard by speaking harshly, you trash their sensitivity and mentally harm them, destroy their receptivity, distance them from you, and disconnect yourself. When you speak sweetly, melodically, poetically, pleasantly, you draw closer to them, the sweetness comes from your attunement to what causes them pleasure, and your sense of identification with them expands. The great performer—artist, opera singer, rock-and-roll artist, actor—opens their heart into vulnerability, and what comes out of their mouth reaches straight through the conceptual defenses of their audience and touches their hearts. Mutual identification occurs, elevating both performer and audience into a self-transcending moment.

When you babble mindlessly, disrespecting the privilege of being with the listener, you lead them into disconnection from reality, into chaos and loss. When you speak meaningfully, you share your own revelations from the insights of enlightened beings—those who have become truly realistic—you share your own realism and you help your listener confront their own reality. Reality is always liberating, energizing, encouraging, though maybe challenging sometimes, and you come together with the listener as you both brace yourselves for evolutionary progress, with your sharing of responsibility in freedom of choice.

The mind is the subtlest but most powerful of the three levels, since it directs the activities of speech and body. Buddhist scientists, not being dogmatists, consider mind in at least two ways in different contexts: both as different in kind from phenomena of the physical level, and also, previously only esoterically, as the most super-subtle of the physical levels. The materialist scientists should like this flexibility of ideology, since it validates materialistic reductionism in some contexts, especially the medical and nowadays the technological. They get more worried about the opposite contexts, where mentalistic or spiritualistic reductionism is also validated and immensely useful—as in developing psychological well-being and unleashing the subtle supernormal powers of the mind, such as clairvoyance, clairaudience, enhanced memory, precognition, telepathy, and telekinesis. It is very important for spiritual philosopher-scientists to recognize the mind as equally approachable as the super-subtle physical, not only in the practical sense that it affects things around you through the instruments of speech and body, but also on the super-subtle energy plane where, through morphic resonance, it acts directly on the super-subtle level of other minds.

Going Deeper into Common Sense

The three mental evolutionary actions in themselves are parallel to the three physical ones—killing/saving, stealing/giving, sexual harm/help.

Hateful, malicious mind thinks destructive thoughts and imagines killing and destroying, and so cuts you off from the larger identification with the living. Loving, benevolent mind imagines union with others, identifies with their lives and wishes their happiness, and expands your own life and evolution.

Covetous, greedy mind wants to take away others' things or even their identities, just like the physical act of stealing, and cuts you off from enjoying their possessions through their doing so, and from mentally rejoicing about others' wealth and beauty (supreme antidote for envy). Generous and freely detached mind enacts a giving action in thought, wanting others to have more and better things, likes them enjoying their things and wants to give them more, and so expands your sense of abundance.

Unrealistic mind disconnects itself and encloses you in the narrow world of self-centeredness—you think you are great, others are nothing (never mind that you are nothing along with them), and you fear and recoil from connectedness, like by doing harmful things with sexuality to create distance even in situations of closest intimacy. Realistic mind embraces causation and connectivity; it not only skillfully reinforces all good qualities and responsible tendencies, habits, and instincts but also enables you to move past fear and expand your connection to the world, realizing the benefit both to yourself and others of open-ing your heart and mind and feeling one with others.

Realistic mind also leads you to discover that the absolute reality of nirvana and all buddhas' reality body is nondual, not separate from the world of causality. It thus enables you to enjoy an immutable deathless bliss virtually beyond causal interference or entanglement, without ceasing actually to engage with the causal world of other suffering beings. The reality of this is inconceivable, stunning, amazing grace, and goes beyond expressibility except for paradoxical statements such as "in but not of the world," "wisdom and compassion indivisible," "bliss-freedom indivisible," and so on.

The great sayings of all world teachers reflect this level of enlightened interconnected consequentiality: "Who lives by the sword dies by the sword!" and even such com-mon sayings as "What goes around, comes around!" All these sayings indicate the common awareness that the way you behave affects your state of being. Ancient people in general, and many people still today, have recognized the reality of the present being affected by happenings in for-mer lives, and so consider how what they do in the present will affect the quality of future lives, just as we normally recognize the effect of prior actions in this life on the pres-ent, and are normally concerned with the effect of present actions on our future in this life.

The Impact of the Karmic Evolution Theory

Buddha as a scientist, once he had perceived the deep-est nature of ultimate reality as free emptiness/engaged relativity, started this conversation with more ignorant beings, explored how beings progress and regress, and elaborated this biological causal theory. He showed beings how to shape life in positive ways and how the supreme form of life is totally blissful and free as an infinitely loving being, fully aware of and merged with all reality. Beneficial to all, a buddha is so blissed out that she or he doesn't need anything more for herself or himself and easily reaches out to include others. She or he experiences as so unnecessary that anyone should suffer in this realm of life that is essentially bliss-freedom indivisible, since even its delusion-driven dimensions are found to be permeated, guarded, and shaped by fully blissful and compassionate beings.

Such is the amazing biological theory of the buddhas. When we catch a glimpse of it, we can quickly see the flaws of the theory of dogmatic materialism, positing that everything consists of mindless atoms and molecules. It's really one big meaningless nothingness, which we can supposedly verify just by destroying our brains or bodies. The fact that we think of ourselves as alive and sensitive is just an accidental trick of atoms and molecules, our genetic coding giving us the delusion of being alive for a purpose. The scientists are seeking to gain full control of this coding so as to make the delusion of existence temporarily more comfortable, until we die. Since this life is a delusion and really meaningless and purposeless, even such a great philosopher as Wittgenstein felt that ethics has no grounding in reality: being good or bad is just a matter of free choice, as there is really no overarching reason to be good or bad.

In Buddha's theory, the way we experience life is delusive because we don't exist in the way we think we do. The way we really exist is as interconnected with a universe of abundant energy that fulfills every need and overcomes every pain and difficulty. We do have the ability to come to understand and experience that, by cutting ourselves free from the knots of the delusions of our alienation. As humans we have the special ability to do that, and indeed we should congratulate ourselves for having achieved the human life-form, which brings us within range of replacing ignorance with wisdom once we confront and realize our true nature.

From a Buddhist perspective, every human has in previous lives been every kind of animal, every animal has been human, and both will be in every other one's form at some future point as well, unless and until anyone becomes a perfect buddha, becoming all of the beings at once, so to speak. It is understandable in some cultures, where people have to treat other species as enemies or as food, that they cannot imagine creatures as sentient. They therefore have no connection with the animal realm. For Buddhist scientists, the great variety of evolutionary life is more like an ocean filled with an infinite variety of struggling forms of life. Buddha differed with the Jains and did not include the plants as sentient beings, saying they don't have the same kind or degree of sensitivity. Of course they are sensitive but perhaps more accepting of where they anchor, put down roots. The difference is not just sentient or insentient, but rather moving or unmoving, migrant or non-migrant beings.

Buddha as a biologist is really a lot like Darwin as a biologist. Both agree about the kinship of humans and animals, and therefore both are strongly resisted by Caucasian monotheists and creationists, who don't want to be connected to monkeys, even genetically, as they are habitually species-ist, racist, and sexist, considering themselves superior to red, yellow, or black humans, and if males, superior to females. Amazingly, in Asia from Buddha's time, although high-caste Brahmins in India and upper classes in other Asian lands resisted the idea of being reborn as lower caste persons or animals, dogs, etc., or worse, they were also overwhelmed (so to speak) by the greater number of beings who adopted the realism of the Buddhist inner scientists and learned to delight in the kinship with the animals. The Indian nations, for example, became more or less completely vegetarian in culture, feeding into the evolutionary action of the day.

So, as mentioned briefly before, there was less resistance to Buddha's karmic biology in India, and it spread swiftly around Asia. People accepted the theory thoroughly. Buddha's karmic biological evolution theory was not widely accepted in India before his time. The general Vedist theory was that the fortunate member of the twice-born upper classes could join the human ancestors in a kind of happy hunting ground after death, and less fortunate persons would simply revert back into the soil to become food for future generations, fortune being determined by the will of the gods, as shaped by the karma of ritual offerings. Buddha's teachings on karma as ethical causation show how actions increase or decrease the quality of one's lives. You become what you do; if you are loving, kind, and generous, then you will become happier, healthier, wealthier, and more beautiful. Though you still might suffer in the short term, due to previous negative actions, if you persist in the positive, the fruit of positive evolution and happier lives is never lost, emerging in the future of that very life or in future lives.

In modern times, there was a famous argument between the well-known anthropologist Ashley-Montagu and the ethologist Konrad Lorenz as to whether the human is basically a social animal or an aggressive one. Buddha (alongside the Dalai Lama) goes with Montagu's argument that the human is basically a social animal. Of course, humans can make horrendous bombs and weapons of mass destruction, using the power conferred by their sociality and language, and so can be far more destructive than other animals. But that comes from the greater intelligence being misused, whereas the actual form of the human bodymind comes from being moral and ethical when living in less intelligent animal embodiments. If you connect this insight to the tenfold path of evolutionary skill or lack of evolutionary skill, you can see how beings can work their way up in tiny, baby-step increments through the forms of the less and less malicious animals. The lion who is less angry with other animals, who has fleeting surges of compassion toward other lions, for example, becomes a less predatory animal in following lives. The human's multi-optional life niche gives it more time and better equipment for skillful action and fun, in fact. Just try to find better-than-human foreplay among the more hardwired, less softwired animals!

In Buddha's theory and laws of evolution, humanity comes from ethical, other-regarding actions, first occurring via tiny surges of sympathy in the mind, and then in expressions, from grunts and mating songs up to articulate speech, and finally in social physical actions. For example, from a karmic evolutionary perspective, if you possess wealth as a human, that comes from past generosity. If you possess beauty, that comes from patience and tolerance, the ability to absorb injury without reactive rage, remaining calm under stress and using skill and strategy to lessen injury all around. Buddha turned away from his birth class of royal warriors and favored the merchant classes, who restrain violence for gain and prosper by fair exchange, living by that relatively win-win approach.

CHAPTER 6

Realistic Livelihood

Once you achieve the realistic worldview and really feel the power of causality, you begin to consciously evolve. You become a conscious evolver! You understand the opportunity and danger of the precious human life. You get determined about your realistic life-purpose motivation. You then feel an existential drive to make your human lifetime count toward making positive evolutionary progress for yourself and others. First, you look upon the power of the word with awe, and commit to always using realistic speech, taking up the educational life on all levels. You intensify your determination to learn everything you can, and you constantly astonish yourself with the fact that you can learn more and more, limitlessly.

You then understand more viscerally the nature of evolutionary skill and begin to shape all your physical, verbal, and mental actions toward the vast openness of enlightenment and away from being closed-minded on any level. Realizing that even your thoughts "evolve" you, you automatically become more mindful and meditative. You surprise yourself moment by moment with the increasing vividness of your experiences.

The final moment of this super-education in living ethically is when you choose your calling or profession with the intention of maximizing your evolutionary progress. In Buddhist societies, such realistic living is close to the mainstream, and the professional mendicant seeker is fully supported. There, the most realistic livelihood means becoming a renunciate mendicant, monk, or nun. But in societies where production and service are the top priorities, there is no such support, and you must choose a livelihood that fits into society well enough and yet optimally enables your quest for enlightenment.

For example, to tell a bit about my own story, once my precious Geshe-lah had read me Nāgārjuna's *Friendly Letter to the King*, I got the four noble truths as friendly facts. What I mean by that is that I sensed the nearness of nirvana combined with the hard work of removing the veils. As a result, I felt there was nothing for it but to become a mendicant monk. I already had been married at a young age and had a beautiful daughter, and upon having to leave that situation on my life quest, I had been living for almost two years as a penniless mendicant, but without the formal vow and professional commitment.

My Geshe-lah understood my determination and acknowledged that I was indeed living like that, celibate and pennilessly dependent on the generosity of others supporting my quest, but he insisted that in the long term I would not be able to live like that, and so refused my urgings that he make me a monk. This went on for the nearly two years of my main tutelage with him, as he maintained that my food and lodging, first at a neighboring Mongolian family's residence and then in the monastery itself, were in compensation for my teaching English to the younger Tibetan monks residing there. Formally speaking, then, I was not being supported by the donations of the monastery's parishioners but was doing a job and receiving sustenance and teachings for that in a mutually beneficial and temporary arrangement.

Toward the end of that two-year period, in late 1964, Geshe-lah finally got tired of my nagging about being a professional mendicant, so he announced he would take me with him to India, where he was going in order to help some elderly Mongolian monks who were stranded there, considered Russian citizens and not eligible for the refugee support the Indian government offered to Tibetan refugees. He told me, "I will leave you there to further study with the Dalai Lama, and maybe he will make you a monk!" In order to go with him, I had to find travel support and financial sustenance for daily living in India, which I was able to beg from my 94-year-old grandfather, who lived with my mother and elder brother at that time.

When we got to India, the 29-year-old Dalai Lama agreed to monitor the studies of the 23-year-old me and eventually decide about my suitability for mendicancy. Though he introduced me as a sincere, smart, dedicated young seeker, 63-year-old Geshe-lah warned the young Dalai Lama, "This nice American boy is very devoted to the Dharma already, and wants to learn as much as he can. He is very capable though a little proud. He really does want to be a monk, but I can assure Your Holiness that he will not be able to stay as a monk for the long term. Nevertheless, I brought him to you, and you are after all the Dalai Lama!"

His Holiness noticed that I was already fluent in Tibetan, so he agreed to take me under his wing, with no further comment about the becoming-a-monk thing. The next couple of years were a great period of learning and bonding with His Holiness, mainly through study arranged with his older teachers, he and I engaging in mutual tutorials, trading Tibetan knowledge for a thumbnail tour in Tibetan of my smattering of high school and college learning. Finally, after a year and a half, his senior teacher, Kyabjey Ling Rinpoche, and he himself agreed to ordain me as a novice and graduate me as a full-fledged mendicant *bhikshu* or Geylong monk—as I had already been living like one for three and a half years. I was overjoyed, and tried to keep every precept with strict observance while redoubling my effort at study and meditation. You could say I had formally found my realistic livelihood, as a professional Dharma practitioner!

Except it was not realistic, as Geshe-lah had predicted. For the next year, it was fine. The next months in Dharamsala were sublime, but then I had to leave due to visa issues. Returning to the American monastery of Geshe-lah in late 1965, I started to have to function as a village priest, so to speak, my studies and meditations interrupted by community service in the form of teaching the children of the Mongolian Buddhist community in the neighborhood. Then some of my young peer American former classmates from here and there began to seek me out. Some of them were involved in the civil rights movement, some in Vietnam War protests, and so on. I tried to help everyone, but mainly I wanted free time to study for eventual Geshe exams in the Indian monasteries and to meditate just for the sake of gaining realization. I served the Tibetan government in exile by traveling with a lama as translator, visiting in Argentina on a mission to establish a Tibetan settlement there—which mission failed for a number of reasons. After some time, I tried to extend my service to my own American community, living here and there with friends or at my family's place in New York.

Ultimately, by the middle of 1966, I woke up to Geshe-lah's practical wisdom. I really didn't fit in anywhere as an Anglo-American Buddhist mendicant without a monastery. In this present life, I was not a Tibetan, I was not a Mongolian. The members of those communities were happy with my interest and growing knowledge, but I was kind of exotic to them; I couldn't really fit as a lama priest among them. I couldn't really serve them in that way, and so it seemed incongruous for them to support me as one of their ministers or priests. There was no Tibetan Buddhist society in Tibet, as the Chinese communists' genocidal ethnocide in the Tibetan homeland was in full swing, desperately trying to prove that Tibet was just a province of China, which had never been the case. And my American peers thought of me as an oddity; I couldn't really help them because, subliminally or overtly, they considered me a lost case, someone who couldn't manage life and was hiding out in some exotic lifestyle. In those days there were no real American Buddhist monasteries, and in any concrete sense I had no realistic livelihood within the culture I had been born in.

So I resigned my robes and sent a letter to His Holiness in India. But I received no reply, since his office in those days was not well organized as now, and even possibly my letter was lost on the way. After a number of ups and downs, I finally realized that the closest thing to a monastery for learning was the university system. The only way I could continue my studies and practices lifelong in American, Protestant-ethic-oriented society was as a university teacher, where I could earn a livelihood by teaching others once I received the necessary professional training as a professor. So I returned to college after my six-year (when I had left in 1961 I wrote "infinite" instead of "in-de-finite") leave of absence, then graduate school, then 50-plus years of further learning and teaching.

Working Out One's Livelihood in Today's Globalizing Society

Obviously, since you know the codes for evolutionary skill, you do not choose to make a living by killing, either directly or indirectly. This makes it difficult to enroll in a military profession, take up food production jobs that involve killing animals, participate in media activities that incite violence by others or that glorify violence and killing, or even consume animal flesh as food or medicine, wear animal skins or furs, or use animal parts as ornaments. You don't want to engage in any business that enslaves people, binds them in some sort of servitude to your profit that ruins their own positive use of their lifetimes, and you don't want to trade in intoxicants that damage their human intelligence and cause them to get into violence and harm themselves or others.

In our modern and complex societies, you also don't want to indirectly participate in killing, say by owning stocks in war machinery companies, voting for aggressive leaders who pledge to destroy enemies, or supporting capital punishment regimes. You even have to be careful of your mind and not allow a secret thought of pleasure in someone else doing something harmful to others, since by vicariously participating in the harm you get a negative evolutionary result.

Just on the first out of the 10 levels of evolutionary skill or harm, it's obvious that it is impossible to avoid killing entirely as long as you are imprisoned in ordinary coarse physicality. Only a pure energy being can come close to avoiding all violence, a being that does not derive its life force from consuming other beings in any way, a being such as an advanced bodhisattva or a perfect buddha. Some of the immaterial dimensions' gods, or greatly creative pure form realm energy gods, come close, but the long-term disembodied states of the former go along with an abandonment of the fates of others, and the huge cosmic whale-like presences of the latter are so huge that they take up energies that might otherwise sustain the lives of others. So neither divine form enjoys the perfection of buddhahood's clearlight immersion in infinite, inexhaustible abundance.

However, Buddha's choice and that of his close mendicant male and female students was to minimize their destructiveness in ordinary reality by living on alms (in the bounteous Indic economy and generous Indian culture), avoiding violence and forms of production that involved violence—by hunting or ploughing, for example. The mendicant lifestyle in societies with the necessary wealth and institutionalized generosity leaves the lightest footprint possible on the ecology of that community.

The basic advice is that you should not be a killer, an assassin, an offensive soldier, an executioner, a weapon maker or dealer, a hunter, a butcher, a robber, a predatory businessperson, a slave seller or owner, a pimp, a liquor maker or seller, a harmful drug pusher, a liar or false advertiser, etc., and that livelihoods that depend on these kinds of harmful acts are therefore to be avoided.

In Buddhist medicine, the ethical livelihood of a person is counted as a positive or negative factor in maintaining or injuring a patient's health, since the human conscience, even if suppressed into being subliminal, has a powerful effect on their overall well-being or lack thereof. In our materialist society where the power of the mind is routinely denied, it is hard to imagine that a person's remote ownership of a war or a meat industry's stocks would make a person evolutionarily liable for the destruction by the weapons made or the suffering of the animals slaughtered, and would lead to a strong though subliminal current of discomfort and even mental depression. But such is Buddhist psychology's claim, and a Buddhist therapist might well counsel someone suffering from depression to liquidate such stocks and invest only in positive enterprises as a way to cheer up, in addition to recommending drugs or lifestyle changes.

Livelihood in the Light of the Five Principles of the Politics of Enlightenment

The fact that the ideal livelihood was to be a transcendent renunciant seeker did not prevent Buddhist science and super-educations from dramatically influencing, even transforming the societies wherein they flourished. As a young scholar and teacher, I was constantly surprised that Americans and modern people in general had such a firm but mistaken idea that Buddhist institutions had no impact on the Asian societies in which they functioned. Looking at the abundance of Buddhist art and literature—and especially at the rock-cut inscriptions of edicts left by the 3rd-century BCE Emperor Ashoka on his famous memorial pillars all over India—I elaborated what I called the "five principles of the politics of enlightenment" as the framework for Buddhist social activism, which drove what I called the "inner revolution" that occurred, to one degree or another, everywhere Buddhism went.

The five principles I discerned in Buddhist social ethical pronouncements, Emperor Ashoka's edicts, and the social advice given to kings in the writings of Nāgārjuna, Āryadeva, Shāntideva, and many others are:

1. Transcendent individualism
2. Nonviolent activism
3. Educationalism
4. Social altruism
5. Monarchically sanctioned egalitarianism or democratism

The first of these five, individualism, comes from the insight that each individual is born alone (except for a possible twin) and dies alone, and the effects of how she or he lives their life are experienced by her or him alone in future lives. Each human individual also has the rare opportunity to fully understand the processes of births and deaths and transcend them into the reality of nirvana and buddhahood, so as to free him- or herself from suffering and so become truly able to help free others to do the same.

The second of these, nonviolence, naturally flows from this principle, since any human life is so valuable to the individual who has it, given the evolution-transcending opportunity to achieve freedom and fulfillment. And this nonviolence should be activist, working nonviolently to put an end to the various violent preoccupations and activities of uneducated societies and individuals. The workings of this process have been hard for historians to notice, since the more nonviolent a society becomes, the more vulnerable it becomes to neighboring societies still addicted to the usual poorly educated but highly trained violent conquest activities. It also becomes a more tempting target because its people become much happier and wealthier, and its lifestyle and infrastructure more beautiful. Its women tend to become more free to demand gentleness and common sense from its less violence-oriented males. Hence such advanced societies have tended to disappear from historians' sight by being invaded and dominated by less advanced peoples. Witness the history of colonialism!

The third principle, educationalism, required making up a new word for the social principle that the best thing for a human being to do is to learn to be a greater human being. (I later discovered to my delight that this word exists in Spanish and Portuguese, with both good and bad connotations, as *"educacionalismo"*!) Along with education being the most important industry in a society, the purpose of human life is to learn, in an endless progression that leads, believe it or not, to full omniscience. Education culminates in "super-education," a path of radical transformation of the individual into a being of love and compassion and universal responsibility for all others—i.e., a buddha, fully awakened and enlightened. In production- and conquest-oriented societies, education is mainly training for a productive or aggressive occupation, designed to aggrandize the wealth and territory and prestige of the society. The lifelong and future-life-oriented education of individuals as the supreme purpose of the collective is the kind of paradoxical principle that is essential to democracy, humorously described by Churchill as "the worst possible system of governance, except for all the others!"

The fourth principle, social altruism, simply means that the society holds the lives of its individual members as sacred—another seemingly paradoxical yet obviously necessary element of any true civilization. Luckily, when any individual becomes super-educated and thereby super-happy, out of gratitude for that, they are courageous and willing to sacrifice themselves for others, for the benefit of a society that values their individuality as supreme above all.

The fifth principle is monarchically sanctioned egalitarianism, which is that the transcendently individualistic, democratic egalitarianism of such a gentle and nonviolent, super-educationalist, and generously socialistic society is best guaranteed by a single enlightened monarch or executive. This preference for monarchy was of course necessary in the Buddhism-influenced history of Asia, though often ensconced within the restraints of councils of minsters or elders. But it may well be something to consider in modern times too, as we have seen that the best social systems have been developed by strong executives even in reflexively anti-socialistic America, such as Franklin Delano Roosevelt. The modern forms of democracy seem to function reasonably well in societies with a symbolic monarch, such as England, Japan, the Netherlands, the Scandinavian countries, and Thailand, where the monarchy can act as a restraint to the oligarchic factionalism that tends to corrupt parliamentary democracies.

The great thing about Buddha's teachings on realistic livelihood is that they were delivered in the context of the relatively civilized Indian culture. Therefore he was able to interact for 45 years with a wide variety of persons and speak with them about how to cultivate a realistic livelihood. Since he had come to understand the deep nature of reality by means of his own reasoning ability and his experiential critical wisdom, he realized that others could realize it themselves. So he was able to dissociate himself from the religions of the time more strictly than other contemporary teachers could.

Coming to a New Understanding

As for how I personally tried to combine realistic livelihood with Dharma practice and further study, I made the
university into my monastery. I love teaching, and I would
say that the teaching experience is a great way to learn.
When you have to explain something to someone who
really wants to understand, you see yourself and your subject in a new light, and you can have new insights. And
perhaps it is the process of your own mind coming to a
new understanding, a deeper insight into some topic that
inspires students to go through their own version of a process of understanding.

But in order to do that, the crucial thing as a teacher is
never to pretend to understand something that you don't.
The deadly temptation for a teacher is, when asked a question, even though you don't really know the answer, to
decide to pretend that you do, because the students expect
it or because you feel you need to maintain your status as
a teacher. I think the key to better teaching is to be completely open with students and to remember that you are
learning along with them. It's much more liberating that
way because you are free to explore new angles or new per-
spectives, or to back down from certain lines of thought,
saying, "I was just thinking out loud, but that is not the
way to get to the answer."

Worldwide Struggles with Realistic Livelihood

In 1950 when the Chinese Communist army invaded Eastern Tibet, the young Dalai Lama fled to the southern border,
poised to go into exile. After some time, against the advice
of his counselors, he decided to return to Lhasa and work
with the Chinese conqueror to minimize the violence of

both the occupier's oppression and his people's resistance. He struggled to do so for eight long years, even going to Beijing in 1954 to negotiate with Mao and Zhou and Deng, and going to India in 1956 to implore Nehru to intervene diplomatically, before realizing in 1958 that he could not, from within the country, stop either the violence of the Chinese genocide or the violent resistance of his people. His version of realistic livelihood could only include work to relieve his people's suffering by escaping into exile in 1959 to speak for them to the world and gradually bring international pressure to bear on China to relent in their oppression. His decisions were invariably both principled along nonviolent lines and pragmatic, given his nation's relative weakness, aiming to minimize the violence, whatever the difficulties and sacrifices required.

Among so-called "Buddhist countries," only some of the Indian nations, Tibet, and Mongolia went so far as to mainstream Buddhistic sciences, spiritualities, and ethics in spite of thereby suffering military and political consequences. However, we should still study their examples in looking at realistic livelihood choices facing us today, on the national as well as individual levels, since the 21st-century situation is novel, perhaps unprecedented in recent millennia.

The planetary situation is that our environment, the irreplaceable basis of our lives, cannot sustain either industrial consumerism or industrial militarism with its horrific technological power. It seems clear enough now that being highly armed and poised for war is no longer survival enhancing. I have a slogan I am fond of repeating, that the nations of our planet must now shift from MAD to MUD: Mutual Assured Destruction to Mutual Unilateral Disarmament. "Mutual" and "Unilateral" are of course contradictory on the surface, but deeper down are both necessary and possible. This might be better understood by imagining two gamblers in a standoff, where each has a gun cocked and wired somehow on the others' temple. If either pulls the trigger, the other's death convulsion will cause their finger to squeeze their trigger, so there can be no winner. Each must, then, while carefully observing the other, extricate the gun from the wiring as the other does, then carefully lower the gun while the other does it in the same timing, bit by bit.

Realistic livelihood today, therefore, must involve the choices of individual self-determination over collective conformity; gentle self-risking over violent self-protection; intensive self-conquest through self-transformative super-education over other-conquest and other-domination, the many caring for every one over each one being dragooned to serve an imagined collective interest determined by dictators (in *Star Trek* terms, the many for the one over the one for the many); and clear tolerance of religious/ideological pluralism and democratic egalitarianism over any form of intolerant orthodoxy and oligarchy.

The Transcendent Virtues

What does developing a realistic livelihood mean in practical terms? Let's go beyond the tenfold skills and elaborate them as a higher degree of positivity by looking at what are known as the bodhisattva transcendent virtues: generosity, ethicality or justice, tolerance or patience, creativity, contemplative awareness, and insightful wisdom.

Generosity is giving things, giving safety, and giving teachings. You should choose a profession that is generous and philanthropic: a parent; a benefactor helping people get out of poverty and gain wealth through making useful things, such as a farmer, carpenter, architect, miner, or technologist; someone who defends people against violence, such as a soldier or security guard; a doctor of body or mind to guard against disease; or a teacher of natural science, about the nature of reality, or of social science, about the nature of societies or of human science, about human nature in general—psychology, philosophy, literature, music, poetry, theater, and so on.

As for the second of the six transcendent virtues, justice or ethicality—you could be a lawyer, a policeman or policewoman, a social worker, a judge, a writer, an honest politician, or a journalist.

As for the third, tolerance and patience—you could be a psychologist, a philosopher, a creative person, actor, or an artist of any kind.

As for the fourth, creativity (I will give more detail on that in the following chapter on the realistic creativity branch), you could work in the arts or in technologies that apply scientific breakthroughs in an ethical way or be creative in any of the vocations mentioned.

As for the fifth transcendent virtue, contemplative awareness—more on this below in the intense concentration chapter—you could pursue artistic professions or spiritual serving in any of the main religious or psychological professions.

Finally, for the sixth, insightful wisdom—you could be any sort of philosopher or scientist pursuing deeper and more accurate understanding of the nature of reality.

The Dalai Lama's Concept of Universal Responsibility

In global terms, the Dalai Lama is the most important of all world leaders, although he is a man without a country. His value can be measured by his urging that his leadership is not important, that all he can say to us is that we must exert our own leadership, and that we must all assume what he calls "universal responsibility" for our own fate and the fate of the earth.

He teaches several key concepts.

First, he stresses the importance and power of science: that we must come to know reality for ourselves through the sciences, not settling only for experts' opinions but trying to learn something and think for ourselves.

Second, he urges us to practice the "common human religion of kindness," the religious and secular spirituality of caring for others as kindly and gently as possible.

Third, he encourages us to take up the sense of universal responsibility: that we must decide that we are responsible for everything, and that this will not exhaust us or give us compassion fatigue or responsibility burn-out, but will keep us toned and active and ready to take on whatever we see needs doing. Part of it is precisely not to use the excuse of being overwhelmed and therefore retreat into being irresponsible. Given a sense of universal responsibility for everything, we can then take up each little thing we see in front of us, and so take it all on in baby steps, bit by bit, moment after moment. It sounds huge, but it's really a matter of not leaving a piece of garbage on the sidewalk next to a garbage can for someone else to deal with; instead we just simply stop, bend down, pick it up carefully, and toss it in ourselves. If we can adopt what I call "the infinite lifestyle" (as opposed to "the terminal lifestyle" of the materialist), we have endless time ahead of us, and we can perfect the universe, turn it into a buddhaverse, bit by bit. That is why these three tenets are excellent methods to keep in mind when cultivating and maintaining a realistic livelihood that will benefit not only ourselves but all of those around us.

CHAPTER 7

Realistic
Creative Effort

The first two branches of the eightfold path, realistic worldview and realistic life-purpose motivation, constitute the super-education in wisdom. The next three—realistic speech, realistic evolutionary action, and realistic livelihood—constitute the super-education in ethics. The last two, realistic remembering/mindfulness and realistic samadhi concentration, constitute the super-education in mind or meditation. The present sixth branch, realistic creative effort (*saṁyagvyāyāma*), is the engine of all three higher educations, though it can also be considered part of the super-education of mind. Remember the six transcendent virtues? Realistic creative effort here in the eightfold path corresponds to transcendent creativity (*vīryapāramitā*) in that bodhisattva set. In both systems it is the opposite of despair, depression, lethargy, laziness, or hopelessness.

Sometimes this is translated as "effort." The reason I translate both terms with "creativity" is that all words for effort—vigor, courage, diligence, enterprise, enthusiasm, etc.—can be used as drivers of negative actions as well as positive ones. You could also be a creative bad guy, killer, or robber, but we usually esteem creativity as creating something good, something beautiful. So our efforts should be expressions of creativity. Creativity is also naturally associated with art and artfulness, making a better world by educating and improving the self as a help to others. All of these move us in a positive direction. This is the sixth branch of the eightfold path.

To review, you might have a breakthrough and be inspired that "buddha is as buddha does!" You realize that creating positive, peaceful, harmonious relations with others in the world is the powerful wave of the supreme good, that ethical actions are super-pleasant, and that you evolve up through joy and benefit yourself supremely when benefitting others. This also grounds you in the first three of those six transcendent virtues of generosity, justice, and tolerance, with their naturally resultant states of super-joy, clearlight transparency, and radiance.

The super-education in ethicality and justice follows naturally, with realistic speech, realistic evolutionary action, and realistic livelihood. All three of these ethical branches are positive evolutionary actions in that they open your being and move you toward the fun of the infinite lifestyle. They become easy and practical, since you don't want to have a way of living that harms others or causes more turbulence in the world, because such turbulence distracts you from the peace of the mind devoted to the positive evolution of self and others.

It is these steps that unblock the fountain of energetic creativity and courageous determination toward complete joy. The result is that we realize that our life is our art, that our art is the boundless love that is the will of the bliss reality, and that it overflows irresistibly and enfolds all others by kindling the inner bliss and beauty they may not have ever been consciously aware of due to the habitual and instinctual error of misknowing ignorance.

Creativity Is Essential to the Good Life

To start, though, we have to realize that creativity is essential to getting something done. In the Buddha's time, he wanted people to start a new way of life, to begin a scientific, psychological, and social ethical revolution—so he encouraged their creativity and mobilized their creative energy.

Before he became Buddha, the buddha-to-be Siddhartha's initial creativity manifested as an explanation to his horrified father as to why he would not take his place on the throne as a king of the Shakya nation. He said something akin to:

"I, Siddhartha, as king could only preside over the ordinary subsistence things. Instead, I am going to seek the higher meaning of human life. My dear father, I will not succeed you as king, since I want to help my people and all people and beings solve their real problems, suffering, sickness, old age, death. I think I can do it! So goodbye! I'll be back, but only when I really know what should be done."

What inspired logic! He essentially said, "Sure, I could help a few people if I took on the role of king, but think of all the people I could help if I overcame the suffering of all beings." If you follow Siddhartha's inspiration here, you will naturally reorder your priorities and make a radical leap out of conventional life, even sometimes entering as he did the mendicant way of life. In modern terms this may look like adopting an educationalist lifestyle. Do nothing but find out what it's all about, and you can easily catch a glimpse of the possibility of a higher reality. You will find people who inspire you. Maybe you'll meet a buddha or someone with traces of such enlightenment along the way.

As you feel freer, you'll develop sympathy for those bound to the wheel of blind duty, and you'll want to get somewhere and be someone who can eventually bring them along too, becoming a bodhisattva in training. As mentioned early on in this book, a bodhisattva is an open or awake-hearted being who strives to benefit all of those around them over the course of multiple lifetimes, until every being is liberated. You might even be inspired to take the bodhisattva vow, to turn your heart inside out and live to benefit all life.

The only prerequisite for being able to do so, of course, is for you to develop a mindset that has the common-sense reality that lifetimes are unlimited and that you have an infinite future ahead of you, and to realize that this future is inevitably related to other beings, forever interrelated with you. And this sense of boundless future must make sense, not just be a wild leap of faith. It involves working to drop out of the conventionally assumed reality of modern culture that life ends in a dying into nothing. Period. Breaking free of such an attitude, even if it's subliminal, is what I call "breaking free from the terminal lifestyle"; and the exuberant sense of freedom that receives you supports your newfound "infinite lifestyle."

The belief that we just end at the time of death is the ultimate killer of creativity. The utterly irrational and un-evidenced belief that something can become nothing is the doorway to despair. You must free yourself of that prison of nihilism to burst into the life energized by altruism—to find the bodhisattva will to optimize reality, to love everyone as much as possible, and to have them love you as you both become enlightened through wisdom, the doorway to creativity. We should all go there and do that before we contemplate too much and escape into artificial detachment. Within the bodhisattva realm, creativity is useful at all levels.

Buddhist Art

Returning to the creativity of Buddha, the first thing he had to do after his blissful enlightenment was to help people try to imagine a world of bliss—the true reality of the third noble truth, nirvana, the cessation of suffering—when all they had ever allowed themselves to experience was suffering. The more intelligent people know full well that temporary, circumstance-dependent pleasures are impermanent and inevitably give way to suffering, frustration, and the addictive search for more pleasures. How could they even imagine such a creative thing as a perfect eternal bliss, something they can personally experience with no sense of loss of their previous embodiment or mind? To open their minds to this reality, inconceivable for them, Buddha had to become an artist, starting with the subatomic-energies-on-up design of his own body and then moving on to the performance art of magical visionary effects, elegant scientific explanations, poetic verses, narrative literature, and so forth, to help people imagine the experience of states somehow suggesting the reality of nirvana.

Similarly, in our more modern times, great art, whether "Buddhist" or not, lifts its viewer, or hearer, or feeler out of their habitual reactions to sense experiences into a melting of habitual postures into beauty, seeing an unexpected higher joy in a quality of "thereness" or "isness" in whatever object they contemplate. It therefore expands the experiencer's ability at first to imagine the inconceivable grace of reality and eventually to experience it.

In individual vehicle Buddhism, Buddha's teaching primarily focused on the priest and warrior classes; he let the mainly male seekers (somewhat chauvinist, self-centered, highly intelligent persons) imagine the bliss of nirvana as a state outside the world. He knew they could not imagine experiencing the world of differentiated objects as configurations of sheer bliss. But they could think of disembodied states of various kinds as possible states of bliss—as perhaps somewhat preferable to, say, a simple state of annihilation. So he taught them, or let us rather say he allowed them, to interpret his teaching as revealing a kind of extinction of embodied experience, a state of nirvana apart from the samsaric cycle. He did hint quite directly that the escapist effort was not the final answer with his teaching of what are known as the "four formless states"—called infinite space, infinite consciousness, nothing whatsoever, and beyond conscious and unconscious—by clearly stating that none of them is nirvana and demonstrating the fact of this in the process of his "dying," by demonstrating a departure from his body into the highest heaven zone of supreme divine embodiment, the Akaniṣhtha, rather than into a formless state.

Before that, even as witnessed in the *Pāli Discourses*, he performed numerous miraculous or extraordinary "performance art" events, such as multiplying his body, levitating to the height of seven palm trees, producing various illusions, manifesting magical emanations, or letting people see different deities that are normally invisible, as when he tripped down a stairway to earth from the Heaven of Thirty-Three with forms of the deities Brahmā and Indra in full view of the humans waiting for him. In various ways, in other words, he creatively expanded their normal perceptions to hint that there was another way of seeing this world.

He also creatively taught students the *Jātaka* tales, the folk-art stories illustrating the ethical good, also teaching a Darwinian-type interconnection between human and animal life-forms—dramatizing for those priest-class male chauvinists that they too had been different genders in previous lives, and even different kinds of animals. He taught that part of his enlightenment experience was his remembering of all his previous lives as different animals and deities, as a bodhisattva messiah-to-be—in that way he introduced the concept of a bodhisattva to his mendicant followers. He did so only hinting that we all have to do the same, refraining from asking most of those sensitive freedom-seeking individuals to undertake such an evolutionary progression over many lives to achieve both release from suffering and full presence to other beings as a buddha. However, to a small circle of advanced students in his universal vehicle assemblies, he didn't hold back the fact that that they too would have to tread the bodhisattva path for countless lives to become a perfect buddha themselves for the sake of others, not only a saint for their own escape from suffering.

In the *Divine Histories* (*Dīvyāvadāna*), there is a story about venerable Upagupta, the fourth leader of the mendicant community after Buddha, that illustrates this artistic effort. Māra—an oft-seen malevolent force or devil in Buddhist lore—distracts the disciples of Upagupta from attending his teachings by putting on a marvelous theater play nearby. After Upagupta loses all his Dharma students to the show, he goes to see it himself and, as the audience is applauding at the end, offers garlands to Māra and his troupe. As soon as the garlands are around their necks, they turn magically into the horrific corpses of dead animals, and Māra and his troupe are unable to flee the magical power of Upagupta. He then makes Māra promise never to put on such plays to distract Dharma students. Māra agrees and says, "Okay, now let us go."

Upagupta says, "Sure, but wait a minute. Before you go, do me a favor. Since you are such a skilled actor, I want you and your troupe to shape-shift and turn yourselves into the Buddha and his foremost disciples, since I never got to meet him many generations ago."

Māra says, "I can do that with my magical show-business powers, but in turn, you have to make a promise to me. When I appear as Buddha, don't get confused and bow to me as if I actually were Buddha, since impersonating him would be a great sin for me."

Upagupta agrees: "Of course I would never mistake you for the Buddha." He then removes the garlands, and Māra and his troupe shape-shift into Buddha and his disciples. Overwhelmed by a joyful feeling of deep faith, Upagupta instantly forgets and bows down with tears in his eyes. Māra cuts this short at once and reverts to his normal form of a bright red god of lust—I call him the "Divine Pimp"—and departs, saying "All promises are off now, since you, venerable, broke your promise to me."

This illustrates the role of art even for the dualistic Buddhists who think they are going to escape the world entirely into another realm and so have no need for art. Of course, sense-objects can be avoided as the snares of the devil Māra, yet they also can bring home the presence of Buddha and the buddhaverse of freedom and beauty and bliss.

In the nondualistic universal vehicle literature, the creative performance art created by Buddha and the bodhisattvas is much more magnificent, even involving the creation of parallel universes, buddhalands (I call them "buddhaverses"), magical jewel trees, and so forth. It even involves temporarily transforming people's bodies into other kinds of bodies, to make a male feel himself to be a female or make a female feel herself to be a male, whatever might help them expand their sense of identification. And in the esoteric Buddhism of the diamond vehicle of the tantras, the imaginative creations of what I call "liberative art" (*upāya*) are even more magnificent.

Today, thanks to the technology of video and computers, artists can create the most extraordinary special effects for an audience, almost lifting them out of their seats and immersing them in the other worlds of sci-fi or fantasy films, or recreating dramatic events from history. In the 1990s, in our effort to get Western people to imagine the reality of Tibet and its material culture before it was invaded—the Tibetan temples and monasteries, aristocratic houses, lama mandala palaces, square kilometers of wall paintings, tangka icons, sculptures, stupas, carved cliff sides, and so on, all destroyed—our Tibet House U.S. in New York did many exhibitions, 11 in different cities all over the world and lots of smaller ones in smaller towns.

But nothing we did would compare to the effect on millions of people of two Hollywood films: *Kundun* by Melissa Mathison and Martin Scorsese and *Seven Years in Tibet* by Jean-Jacques Annaud. The first depicts the life story of His Holiness the Dalai Lama from birth to his escape to India; the second, the recreation of the adventures in Tibet of the Austrian mountain climber Heinrich Harrer. These films multiplied a millionfold the effect of getting Western and free Asian people to fall in love with the beauty of Tibet.

Art as All Methods of Liberating
Beings from Suffering

Art in its broadest sense is the technique and activity and product of doing something skillfully beneficial. The Sanskrit word *upāya*, which many people translate as "skillful means," or "method," or "strategy," or even "trick," I translate as "art," as in "the arts and sciences" taught in the university. And so "artistic skill" is what Buddha or bodhisattvas are demonstrating when they produce a special effect, give a particular teaching, or make a particular show. They are doing what I call "liberative art." And this is why art has always been the central manifestation of Buddhist compassion. The cinematic art of Hollywood at its best is another powerful step in this tradition, with a truly global impact.

Buddhist culture and thought also offer an art-critical criterion for what is good art and what is bad art. Bad art is advertising or propaganda, which merely puts lipstick on a pig, so to speak, where the samsaric cycle is made to seem glamorous and attractive by being falsified. For example, some films use gratuitous violence to excite or pornographic eroticism to attract, but do not show the true destructiveness of war and violence or the earthy, gentle, and peaceful side of the erotic, which may be ecstatic but is not always glamorous.

Good art comes from the heart of the artists, where they are lifted beyond themselves, where they are not seeking either profit or fame and have no manipulative agenda. They are simply evoking their own vision of something deeper and more beautiful, more funny, more amazing, or more horrific, and this then moves the hearts of the audience. It is expressed in Buddha's universal vehicle theory as what is called the "artistic emanation body" (*shilpanirmānakāya*), where the artist loses herself or himself in their act of creation and is taken up in the emanation body of all buddhas and becomes a channel for conveying to their audience the possibility of liberation and the joy of pure and amazing grace.

Solving the Planetary Crisis with Creativity

Creativity is certainly most needed now to meet the challenge of the current world crisis, where a culture based on materialism—mindless mechanism of material forces and substances—must adapt to the reality that the seemingly intangible forces of human minds are so powerful in the forms of greed and hatred that they are disrupting all the mechanisms and material processes of nature.

Great scientists and adepts have worked for 1,300 years to build a Tibetan Buddhist culture so powerful that even non-Buddhists take inspiration from it. That's why I take the time to show that *upāya*, one of the transcendent deeds of the bodhisattvas, like realistic creative effort (*samyagvyāyāma*), our sixth branch of the eightfold path, implements the power of compassion through the art of liberating deluded beings. A suffering being first must imagine being happy in order to be motivated to seek happiness. And it is art that lifts the suffering being by providing a sense of relief and then giving them hope that there could be happiness.

For example, the Buddhist teacher Tsongkhapa, during the long retreat that led to his full enlightenment in 1398, went and refurbished the temple to the future Buddha Maitreya. Later, he called a congress to renew the *Vinaya* discipline rules for the monks, the guiding principles of their culture, also forming a foundational ethical core for lay people. On the 1409 lunar new year, he founded the great prayer festival for all forms of Buddhism in order to make it culturally mainstream and central in Tibet. Finally, he built exquisite 3D gilt bronze mandalas in a specially built esoteric hall in his Ganden monastery to anchor the tantric bliss-freedom-indivisible reality at the heart of Tibetan culture. Since then the Dalai Lamas have continued this tradition. His Holiness our Great 14th Dalai Lama, in exile and therefore present all over the world, attends to the art institutions—monasteries themselves having huge "art faculties," if you will, which are the tantra faculties. Tantra is super-art, actually.

Once, during a public conversation on art between the Dalai Lama, Richard Gere, and Alice Walker, I noticed that the Dalai Lama's interpreter translated English "art" into a Tibetan word meaning only paintings and sculptures—causing His Holiness to say he knew nothing about it so they should talk among themselves! Later, when I caught up with His Holiness, I told him in Tibetan, "Your Holiness, please don't say that you don't know what 'art' is. I know you're thinking it refers to some paintings, or maybe music. But 'art' really means *upāya* (*thabs* in Tibetan), the seventh transcendent virtue, which expresses the compassion released by the sixth, which is wisdom. So 'art' really means the way of creating anything that lessens beings' suffering! Your Holiness's whole life is a total work of art. The biography of Buddha is called *Lalitavistara*, which means 'The Magnificent Play,' almost like 'The Greatest Show on Earth.' So please don't say you know nothing about it! Your Holiness, you know everything about art!"

He was pleased. "Realistic!" he said.

The reason the Dalai Lamas were especially focused on art—in the sense of *upāya*, ways of summoning the imagination to inspire people to seek liberation—is that Tibet was the first culture that made Buddhism mainstream, no longer merely countercultural as it has been almost everywhere else. After a thousand years of development, it became mainstream with the advent of the "Great Fifth" Dalai Lama. And as Tsongkhapa showed, art was the key for making Tibet's unique, what I call "mass monastic," culture the mainstream. It was a tour de force, setting a clear historical example of the effective art of transforming a nation's mainstream culture from imperialist militarism to monastic transcendentalism.

Creativity as Art in the Advanced Esoteric Level

This brings us to the vajra vehicle, which is the creative tantric esoteric aspect of the universal vehicle known as the Mahayana.

The *Kālachakra "Time Machine" Tantra* contains the legend of Shambhala, a hidden land of normal humans near the North Pole, wherein the people have become so transformed and gentle through tantric subconscious-self-transformation that it is safe for everyone to be open and vulnerable. In its legend, it has a series of 32 kings, the last 25 of whom are called Kalki kings—which I translate as "Democratic" kings, because the sixth king initiated the whole population into the *Time Machine Tantra*. He then commanded that henceforth they were all "diamond" (*vajra*) yogic individuals, and that every other citizen was a "diamond" brother and "diamond" sister to every other, so there would thenceforth be no more caste hierarchy but only a single "diamond" caste—all would be in principle equal.

The last of the Kalki kings of Shambhala has to deal with an invasion, which he repels; he then proceeds to spread democracy and spiritual freedom all over the entire planet. People who feel insecure in the universe and therefore become addicted to power are afraid and naturally think everything is just there for their own benefit—they fear democracy. Mammals give an altruistic push toward community while humans are more vulnerable among species, and for humans democracy is perfect, with its primary purpose being the education of each person to reach their full altruistic potential in enlightenment.

Tantra began to come out of secrecy in India by the middle of the first millennium of the common era. By then it was safe enough, as the land had become somewhat monasticized, and thus demilitarized, and educated. Women were more appreciated and treated better, though still not equal. At any rate, more people were able to seek beauty. Larger masses of people could feel greater individual energies and remain gentle, turning to education, art, and culture to undo emotional and neurophysiological armoring and to lessen the emotional plague of psychological constriction, frustration, and cruelty. Such was the progress of the cool social revolution throughout Indic history since Buddha's time.

As can be felt at an Indian rāga concert, or in bhakti devotionalist chanting, Indian societies had become more relaxed and organized to allow more people to be vegetarian, to let the heart feel easy, surrender more easily to realities, and be vulnerable and open to joy in both earthly and spiritual ways. There were still the monotheistic authorities, still their military thing, still too much of the grip of that. But the psychonauts, the great adepts, were so powerful as individuals that they were able to take all three vehicles—individual, universal, and diamond apocalyptic levels of creativity—to Tibet, Japan, and Indonesia, where they might be preserved through the second-millennium ordeals of barbarian conquests and invasions and regressive authoritarian social styles.

In the 1,300 years of the Tibetan mainstreaming of the openhearted, gentle culture, we can see a number of 11-generation, two-century-long steps of change. First the emperors brought in the monastic universities, taming the warrior fixations holding up the conquest society, using top-down authority to educate the people, thus undermining the strength of their own top-down authority. Then there was a period of atavistic resistance to the more peaceful culture, which shut down the monastic universities, though it couldn't stop the grassroots dissemination of the new education. This period from circa 840 to 980, during which the empire collapsed, was poorly documented, but the tantric yogi psychonauts were surely active underground with lay practitioners.

Then regional kings teamed up with monastic university abbots for a couple more centuries, 980 to 1150, during which time the spiritual leaders became so powerful that they led the entire nation's response to the Mongol empire. In the period from 1150 to 1390, the new generation of adepts began the process of extending the "taming" or civilizing process to the wild Mongolian conquerors while getting the Tibetan lords themselves more and more used to not having much military power, since under the Pax Mongolica, no one challenged the Mongolian armies.

The next step was mass monasticism spreading over the entire plateau from 1400 to 1580, with the huge monasteries serving as transformative universities for creatively educating larger and larger numbers of people in the sciences and arts derived from the curriculums of the great Indian monastic universities. This period culminated in what can only be thought of as a kind of reverse Reformation in the late 16th and early 17th centuries, when another overwhelming Mongolian force helped the Great

Fifth Dalai Lama make Tibet's own aristocratic militarists finally succumb to the monastic universities, allowing the head lama of all the biggest universities to take responsibility for ruling the whole plateau. This resulted in the Great Fifth's building of the Potala, and the Tibetan people coming to feel that their savior figure, the bodhisattva Avalokiteshvara, was committed to a continuous human reincarnation as their political as well as spiritual leader.

This was the nature of "modern" post–17th century Tibet, where the Buddhist education movement became the mainstream focus of human lives and everything was rationalized around that individual evolutionary purpose. This does not mean that everyone became enlightened or that Tibet was Shambhala (or Shangri-la)—far from it. There were many unenlightened Tibetans, many imperfect people in the universities, and considerable complacency in the spiritual communities. But everyone, however imperfect, understood that the main purpose of life was to advance toward buddhahood, that many individuals had in fact achieved that goal, and that any individual who made the full effort could do so successfully. Therefore all individual and social creativity was aimed that way, directly or indirectly.

Thus, in the monastic university and in its advanced tantric colleges and postgraduate retreat community institutes, creative effort went beyond educating the conscious mind to see the beauty of the buddhaland and intensify the awareness of the immediate presence of nirvanic experience in the here and now. Many individuals put their effort into the internal science of tantric transformation, contemplatively deploying yogic arts to dissolve what the pioneering Western psychologist Wilhelm Reich called individual "emotional armoring" in order to open toward the blissful fruition of buddhahood, for the sake of all other beings within their field of artful activity.

The tantras creatively used a neuroscientific patterning of the central nervous system into a subtle body system of channels, energies, and neurochemical essence drops. The yogi practitioners had already realized the plasticity of all identity structures through the physics of voidness and relativity, and so could regularly shift out of a coarse body self-identity into a subtle body of patterns, circulatory energies, and fluids in order to consciously—lucidly—traverse the layers of consciousness from waking to sleeping to dreaming, though life, death, the between state, and the conscious reincarnation process.

Thereby they followed their Indic psychonaut ancestors and mastered the dying process to learn to die lucidly, rehearsing the whole range of "near-death" experiences without actually harming their coarse bodies, traversing the luminous and radiant mind states reachable by contemplative adepts. They probed even beyond into the super subtleties of the clearlight energy field wherein death is experienced as the essential energy of life. They carried the Indic researches even further than the Indic psychonauts had been able to do, due to the relative isolation of their high plateau and the sheer numbers of practitioners relative to the size of the population.

The amazing creativity they thus unleashed reflected on the popular level in the famous "Book of the Dead" literature, which enabled quite a number of people to reach buddhahood itself. These practitioners obtained the adept ability to embody themselves without feeling apart from the clearlight of the void. No expression can encompass this "clearlight of the void"; it is super-subtle, at a level where there is no duality of body and mind, where super-subtle mind is the same as the super-subtle body, in the plane of inconceivable subparticulate energy, wave-particle nondual energy, welling up on demand from the super-calm, inexhaustible, infinite clearlight energy. This is the quiescent but inexhaustible fountain of true creativity, available to a buddha, a being who is the conscious agency for shaping coarse realities of embodiment.

Creativity Emerges in Buddhaland Building

There is a story that illustrates the creativity I am speaking of, as taught in the *Vimalakirti Teaching Discourse*. The *Discourse* text begins with Buddha residing in the mango grove of the famous actress Amrapali outside the wealthy Indian city of Vaishali. A group of yuppies come out for a visit and are moved to offer their jeweled parasols when they enter Buddha's field of easy presence. Buddha then does a piece of performance art and fuses the parasols into a kind of planetarium, which surrounds the audience and imparts a vision of the total interconnectedness of galaxies, planets, tapestries of alternate universes, and all their heavens, mountain ranges, continents, oceans, river valleys, towns and cities, heavenly and earthly and underground animal realms, and so forth. The youth are amazed at the vision and sing Buddha's praises in very intelligent verses. They then ask the Buddha the creativity question:

> "O Blessed One, we heard your teaching, we are already on our way to unexcelled perfect enlightenment, with the bodhisattva motivation to learn the worldview, the ethicalities, and the meditations. But what we want to know is how do you create the buddhaverse? How do you make it beautiful?"

Buddha first responds that it is impossible to build a buddhaland or buddhaverse, because all is empty, but that is why a bodhisattva goes ahead and builds one. It's impossible because everything is relative, and even a buddhaland is illusory (here we must remember that whenever a buddha negates something that seems real, such as your eye, or ear, or nose, he is only negating its *intrinsic* reality, not its relative presence). Then he proceeds to teach that the world here and now is already a buddhaland; it is the one Shakyamuni has already built as a theater in which beings can find the optimal conditions for evolving toward their own enlightenment, freedom, and bliss. After he finishes his description of the land, he is challenged by Shāriputra, one of the foremost of his dualist, individual vehicle disciples, in response to which he bestows a momentary vision of this land as an ideal teaching environment. The creativity of a buddha's compassion is thus presented as being able to transform the environment, not just the interior of the individual.

A buddhaland in a buddhaverse is thus designed to provide beings with a perfect evolutionary situation to maximize evolutionary achievement of their lives, with the human life-form being the most sensitive and intelligent of life-forms, capable of using such an environment in the most effective evolutionary way. Imagining the world to be like this puts people into a sense of empowerment: "Yes I can, I can do it, I can evolve! I can understand emptiness and the relational self as a continuous work of art. I can make the creative effort to make everything more beautiful and build, purify, and transform the world into a buddha world."

This is what happens when you have a sense of the axiality and centrality of yourself in the buddhas' omnipresence. After all, a buddha is defined as a reality body;

her/his real body is all reality filled with both animate and inanimate beings and things. So s/he feels totally responsible for the misknowledge-created world, with its creative gods and every kind of being, all tending to suffer under the power of not knowing that the real world is the uncreated primordial nirvana play of bliss-freedom indivisible. S/he exercises his or her responsibility spontaneously and effortlessly, opening her- or himself as a portal of the infinite energy of relativity to energize all beings and things everywhere to become creative themselves, discovering their own wise and skillful love-power to enjoy and offer beauty to whatever degree they can and the environment around them can bear.

Another way to think of this form of creativity is to consider people who perceive the world as filled with horrors; they are simply projecting the horrors of their own misknowing and addictive minds upon the buddhaverse of natural perfect beauty. Of course, mystics of all traditions in this world, and also many simple persons in their inexpressible, astonishing deeper experiences of grace and blissful communion, all intuit this reality, calling it by whatever names are available in their cultures. The experience of communion within the reality body of infinite wisdom and love does not belong to "Buddhism" at all.

This change in view encourages creativity within one's own mind, where one can bring into focus the wisdom and ethical super-educations activated at this point. When you turn your awareness inward, you begin to see reactions and habits, with distracting and negative thoughts bubbling up out of you-don't-know-where. This is when you can turn your creativity to editing those thoughts and finding the wellsprings of wisdom, love, compassion, and beauty in your own mind. This then brings you into the region of remembering, also known as mindfulness, which is exploring your conscious/unconscious boundary to become fully and totally conscious, hence able to steer your mind—and through it your actions—into better and better joyful creativity.

So once the creative energy of your own mind focuses on the seminal super-subtle realm accessible only by the coarse, subtle, and super-subtle mind, you turn to the third super-education: the education in mind and in samadhi, the supernormally empowering mental concentration that reshapes the world into continuous beautiful loving art by reshaping the mind into the bliss-overflowing awareness that lovingly enfolds all embodiments. We'll begin with realistic mindfulness.

CHAPTER 8

Realistic Mindfulness

The super-education in mind begins when your creativity flows inward into the subtlest recesses of your mind. This can be called "mindfulness," forms of which have become extraordinarily popular around the world. The English "mindfulness" comes from the Sanskrit *smṛti* (Pali, *sati*), which actually means "memory." Among the eight branches of the path, it is the seventh, the beginning of the third super-education, the super-education in concentration (*samādhi*) or mind (*citta*). Realistic remembering and realistic concentration make up that third super-education, with what we discussed in the last chapter, realistic creativity, as the spark.

Together they parallel the fifth of the six transcendent virtues, contemplation (Sanskrit *dhyāna*, Chinese *ch'an*, Korean *son*, Japanese *zen*), which partners with the sixth and most important transcendent virtue, wisdom (*prajñā*).

The transformative intellectual wisdom attained by analytic meditation (*vipashyana, vipassana*) cannot drill down far enough to change unconscious, misknowing habit-patterns without the energy-focusing of concentration, contemplation, nondiscursive meditation, or realization (Sanskrit: *samādhi, dhyāna, shamatha,* and *bhāvana*).

Usually our constant stream of "remembering" gets stuck in the past as we go into reveries in our memories of what happened to us at this or that time, and the same type of mental scattering occurs in anticipating things, where we imagine things that might happen in the future—we "remember" the future. When we take focus away from remembering the past and anticipating the future, we can "remember" to be more and more aware and mindful of what is going on in the present. When we do this, indeed, we can gradually become lucidly aware.

To look at it from a different perspective, we use a term—*lucid dreaming*—when we have learned to be self-aware during dreams without waking up. When we gain skill in mindful awareness during our waking hours, we are developing "lucid waking," finding much more vivid detail in every moment. If we take stock of how we spend our time, doing things while our mind multitasks and thinks about other things, scattering itself around, we are hardly aware of what we're actually doing in the moment; that could be called "mindless waking" or "sleep-waking."

There are traditionally four focuses of mindfulness, of "remembering the present":

1. Remembering the body
2. Remembering the physical and mental sensations
3. Remembering the mind
4. Remembering mental objects

You can practice a first round just to become aware of them, without looking right away at their nature. Once you become lucid about what is there, you discover that the body is funky, the sensations are mostly stressful, the mind is ever-changing and actually unfindable, and mental objects are coreless, insubstantial, illusory, and relative. "Realistic mindfulness" constantly looks realistically with the inner eye at body, sensations, mind, and objects.

Popularly in the West people think of "mindfulness" as being mainly one aspect of the mindfulness of the body, which is mindfulness of the breath, breath being considered the bridge between mind and body. So when you first do mindfulness practice, you get a little nervous because you realize there's a whole cacophony going on inside your mind. But then once you get to see it more comprehensively, and you can move around among your thoughts, you develop a little bit of critical awareness, and you can change channels. You have a sort of clicker. You finally get a remote control in your own mind and you can click from one channel to another. You can look at it from another angle and get another perspective on it. And you can be more free about your reactivity. When someone presses your button, you can either react or not react because you're not a slave of that thought. You can shift away from it.

Mindfulness is a technique developed by centuries of mind science in practice. The most important thing determining the quality of your life is your mind and your own ability to master your mind. You can be in the best environment and something bothers you emotionally and you're miserable. You can be pretty happy even in adversity. Mindfulness gives you a much bigger range of choice and an ability to create gaps and pause your reactions so you can choose to move this way or that way. It's really very important.

One practice is to heighten awareness of the inner complexity that normally functions automatically: the workings of the body, for example. This is how most people who get into mindfulness do it, performing a nonjudgmental inner opening of awareness as to what is actually going on inside the body and mind. The natural deeper step of critically seeing through your body's pseudo-purity, your mental sensations' pseudo-pleasantness, your seemingly static, ego-centered mind's pseudo-static fixity, and your pseudo-solid objects of mental experience happens when you go beyond the soothing calm of non-judgmental awareness and become lucid and naturally begin to transform. This is the deep meditation in which the insights from learning and critical investigation are ready to be catapulted by samadhic total concentration to lift you out of the coarse bodymind world into the subtle space of natural reality bliss.

Buddhist psychological science starts from the second noble truth or friendly fact, which focuses on the diagnosis of the cause of suffering: misknowing ignorance. "Misknowing" ignorance causes unawake beings to imagine their selves and their world as being other than what they really are. Such beings (I still am somewhat one of them, so don't feel put down!) are like the hero Neo in the film *The Matrix*, who thinks he is a certain body running around in a certain world. When he is caused to "remember" (become self-aware as awakened by technical intervention), he realizes that he is actually an unconscious, dream-trapped, embryo-like grown-up trapped in a slimy test-tube prison. Luckily, his already awake revolutionary new friends save him as his body gets flushed out to die in a sewer due to his crime of having become unmanageably self-aware.

This is a beautiful illustration of the initial awakening from misknowing into the gradual learning of mindful knowing. Once you misknow yourself as an alienated, separate being surrounded by the misknown immensity of an absolutely "other" world, you crave to lose that separateness by uniting with that world. This may look like you are swallowing it as much as possible or being swallowed totally by it, lust driving you to avoid alienation and fear driving you to avoid contact. At the same time, you may fear both not being able to swallow it all and also being swallowed by it, so you rage against it and lose yourself in hatred, anger, and aggression. The original misknowing of the separation, of course, is the root of both the lust and the hate.

When the fully awakened Prince Siddhartha became Shakyamuni Buddha and taught his first human disciples, his five former self-mortifying yogic companions, he emphasized lustful craving as the cause of suffering in order to shock them. They thought they were torturing themselves to get rid of craving, but they were actually doing the opposite: craving escape from reality, seeking a separate state of being by retreating into the illusory experience of the totally misknown, mis-imagined, static, separate, absolute self, thought to be disconnected from the bothersome relative world.

When Siddhartha attained enlightenment, he lightened up, felt both body and mind to be really well. To be precise, he became nirvana, all free, all bliss, all the time, everywhere, as everything. He did not fail to be himself; he just came to know what he had really been all the time. He expanded from identifying himself as a static self, separate from all time and space full of beings and things, to identifying himself as still himself, astonishingly just forever completely one with the whole time and space full of beings and things. That is to say, although this was inconceivable in normal terms, he came to be all other beings and things just as much as continuing to be himself.

As soon as he found that to be who he really was, he recognized that it was not as if he had changed from one thing into another; he simply came to know what he had always been. His sense of himself as separate—a piece of live physicality, separate from its environment and other beings with a separate self-essence somehow contained within that physicality—was mistaken. It was ignorance, misknowledge. Once wisdom cleared away misknowing's hold over his awareness, he could simultaneously remember how he felt under misknowledge, realizing how it had always been an illusion, and also know and enjoy that the bliss of release had always been who he really was. He realized that he had always been enjoying it as his actual nature, while his mind was kept unconscious of the fact by habitual misknowing.

I know this is impossible—to realize two opposite things at once—which is why nirvana is said to be inconceivable and inexpressible, beyond words. It is a sustaining awareness that embraces extreme cognitive dissonance with blissful ease.

Impossible though it may be, we already do such a thing all the time. The best example is when you look at your face in a mirror. You see a face "in there," like yours except left-right reversed. If you had never done so, you might reach into the mirror to touch the face there, surprised when your hand bumps into the glass surface. After you have that surprise, you know it is only an illusion, a reflection of your own face. You continue to see it in just the same way and yet you simultaneously know it is not as it seems, but an illusion on the surface of the mirror. Without any strain you maintain the two knowings, that of the 3D image out in the room beyond the mirror window and that of its illusoriness. You simultaneously reconcile the cognitively dissonant awarenesses of your face as both being there and not really being there.

Ignorant misknowing awareness (*avidya-asatvidya-vidya*) dooms us non-buddhas to the suffering of living in a mirror reflection world that seems to be evidently apart from us. This is more misknowledge than ignorance, since you actively think you know something that is not real to be real. This is the basic cause of your suffering. You think you know a certain environment and world, and you try to live in it, but you keep banging into its mirror reflection unreality. You know you are in some reality, but you are unconscious of it, so you are always anxious and insecure.

The shocking fact is that Buddhist psychology shows us that any unawake, suffering person is diagnosable as virtually "psychotic" in today's psychological terms, as they are suffering from a psychosis defined as a lack of contact with reality. To the extent that you are unenlightened, you are living in an unreal world created by your misknowing-distorted psyche, which makes you, technically, psychotic.

Don't take it personally; I am not yet fully enlightened either so I am happy to join you there! But it is a big relief to know the diagnosis, as it gives me hope that I can practice realistic remembering and be cured of my misery. Buddhist psychological science provides me with that diagnosis. It also presents me with the super-positive prognosis that my suffering is curable in nirvana, which is inalterably my real reality, experientially reachable by a comprehensive, therapeutic super-education.

As one of the psychotics myself, I think I'm in a world that isn't the real one, but to begin to correct my psychosis, it helps to know I'm misknowing. I'm still in it, I think, still suffering in 2021 CE New York, on Turtle Island, or the North American continent, planet earth, in our solar system and galaxy and nebula. I believe myself to be in a coarse physical body, an entity different from other beings and the other things—the table, floor, walls, ceiling, and computer. I habitually think I'm really me, and the other, the world, is really something different. I am what Buddhist psychology calls an alienated individual (*Pṛthagjana*).

I act on the world, reaching out to people through an envelope of disconnection, my inner psychosis causing me to absolutize people and the world around me as completely different, making everything unnecessarily problematic, and leading to a tendency to not take responsibility for myself.

Once we can move beyond denial and diagnose ourselves in this way, our creativity emerges into mindfulness. We are encouraged to be more realistic about ourselves, to be mindful of what we actually are, open to the possibility that we have been misknowing ourselves.

Now let's follow the mindfulness or remembering source, the *Great Focus of Mindfulness Discourse*. Though this is a witness of the Buddha's direct discourse, it is not at all religious. It is only therapeutic, a doctor's leading of the patient through a specific therapeutic protocol.

You decide to educate yourself in mind, so you assume the position of balanced sitting, either in a chair or cross-legged on a cushion. You can sit with your back straight, hands folded in your lap. Your mouth can be gently closed with your tongue touching your palate, your chin slightly tucked with the neck relaxed, shoulders square straight, and your eyes half-lidded and focused just beyond the tip of your nose.

You are going to focus your mindful awareness on your body, where "you" are located, to become lucidly awake about being it. You start by focusing on your breath, the bridge between body and mind. You breathe normally through your nostrils and count your breaths on exhalation from one to ten. You will almost at once notice that a train of thought will take you away from the counting before you get very far, and in that moment, your mindfulness kicks in. You "remember" you are practicing mindfulness, so you let go of the train of thought, dismount from it, disidentify from it being you, and come back to "one" with the exhalation of that moment. Don't cheat yourself by resuming from wherever you remember you had reached, be it two or three, or higher. Go back to one. No one is judging your failure to concentrate on the counting; actually, your success is your noticing your mind being distracted by a thought-train coming out of your unconscious; you dismount from the thought-train and refocus your concentration on the breathing.

As you continue, you may find you are more and more successful, in that you become aware of more and more distracting thoughts, and of distracting thoughts about the distracting thoughts, and all sorts of funny memories bad and good, and also many anticipations or anxieties, imagining future good or bad scenarios. This is a stage where if you have not learned something of the inner science about the processes, the benefits and dangers of practicing and not practicing, awakening and not awakening, you may become discouraged and turn to thinking of yourself as a hopeless case, a non-meditator, and decide it doesn't work for you and give up. You will lose your inner creativity and decide you can't change the way your mind is and it's just another bother to you. You secretly or vocally feel bad, lose your self-confidence, and become depressed.

Mindfulness begins just by watching your thoughts and learning to see how they rise and fall. It is not a project to identify with one particular inner voice as your controller, but rather a way to find your inner freedom. You can even attain states of thought-free concentration, through the path of serenity (*shamatha*), which creates a kind of elation and bliss and is a sign of fluent fitness of mind to focus on any object you want. Because such a state is not too hard to attain, some might think that just being thought-free is enlightenment, perhaps the goal of all practice. This is a misunderstanding, with a bit of a danger in it. The point is rather to gain inner freedom, become aware of your inner reactivity, make decisions about reacting or not reacting to inner thoughts and impulses, and then choose what you are going to manifest. In other words, don't believe everything you think!

Back to mindfulness of the body, the first of the four focuses of mindfulness. In the *Great Focus of Mindfulness Discourse*, there is a long list of all the components of your physical body. You scan your entire physique— your skeleton, muscles, ligaments, circulatory system, blood, lymph, interstitial fluids, nervous system and its electrical impulses, organs and vessels and their contents, brain, sense organs and their fields, including the mental sense organ and its inner field—but not yet in too much detail. You might get down to cells, molecules, atoms, sub- atomic particles, and energies, but not pushing too finely into pinning anything down. Just trying to be aware of everything. You realize you are a conglomerate, highly imperfect, changing, actually somewhat indeterminate set of processes, but you don't push on it. You just want to remember, be lucidly aware of what you are, in as fine detail as possible.

What happens as you stabilize this focus is that you end up floating in your sensations. You realize you cannot be certain, cannot fix your bodily solidity; it keeps slipping away from your awareness of it. This then naturally induces you to turn to the second of the four focuses of mindfulness: your sensations. Traditional accounts translate Pali or Sanskrit *vedana* as "feelings," which is misleading. These are not emotions—reactions to sensations—but the sensations themselves, both physical and mental, merely the noticing of pleasure, pain, and numbness. For example, you could focus on your knee—its joint, ligaments, skin, muscle fibers, down to cells and molecules—and then you reach mentally to feel the sensations of it being your knee. You might end up feeling a pain from sitting cross-legged, still, in a fixed posture. There may be some pleasure in feeling your pant leg smooth on the skin. You feel nothing much from some of the surfaces you can imagine around the knee. Your mind senses discomfort at sitting still while it hurts, and some comfort at being able to sit still anyway, holding your meditative pose. You move around with your mind through all the complex sensations, mental as well as physical, inventorying the visual, audial, olfactory, gustatory, and tactile sensations, a kind of cloud of mental states, sort of surrounding the physical structures you held in the first mindful focus. These sensations of pleasure, pain, or numbness are the way the mind seems somehow to contact the physical.

As you try to stabilize this second focus, your mindfulness naturally pushes toward the third of the four focuses of mindfulness, the focus on your mind itself. It seems less and less concrete and unitary the more it looks at itself. As you investigate the mind, it becomes scattered into components: fleeting cognitions of visual, audial, olfactory, gustatory, and tactile objects, interspersed with awarenesses of surges of desire, hate, delusion, and the fading of those distractions. This focus of your mind on itself may cause you to feel confused, maybe even a bit dizzy or faint, as you get lost in the complexity of your conscious-ness. And this naturally leads you into the fourth focus of mindfulness: the realm of mental objects.

You begin to realize that all of your mindfulness focusing has been dealing with mental objects; indeed, your body awareness was filtering the spray of your sensa-tions of your bodily parts and components through a set of inner images of your anatomy, ideas of your body parts and constituents. You realize that your mind functions in a cloud of images and ideas and emotional reactions, driven to maintain its sense of existence and purpose and direction by an inner narrative or alternating sets of narratives.

Having explored the four focuses of mindfulness, you then become aware of hindrances to your lucid awake-ness. These are the five hindrances of craving, annoyance, depression, agitation, and confusion. Your awakeness alerts you to their presence, how they are seen through and so fade, and how they are precluded by sustained focus. The mindfulness of these leads to insight, which goes beyond mere awareness of their presence to seeing through them, reaching a natural detachment from their presence by abandoning constant grasping at their presence, thereby feeling at ease and free within the mind.

Then Buddha leads his patients through impos-ing numerous schemes on the host of mind-objects, organizing them conceptually into the five aggregative processes—physical, sensational, conceptual, emotional, and cognitive—and then becoming lucidly awake about them, then insightful, then letting them go. Next he leads them into analyzing their consciousnesses themselves as visual, audial, olfactory, gustatory, tactile, and mentally sensed interior fields known as the twelvefold sense-fields within consciousness. He leads them again to gain insight.

By now we the patients are more and more detached from obsession with inner phenomena, our minds tending to feel meditatively disembodied, in fact. So he leads us to develop a kind of subtle mental body made of the seven enlightenment components: mindful awareness itself, critical discernment, creativity, delight, calm, concentration, and equanimity. Insight and lucid wakefulness come about when using this scheme, and there is a sense of inner freedom and detachment that is even stronger than before.

This last focus of your mindfulness is on things in the mind, your mind-objects. The last of the lists of things in your mind is the four noble truths, or friendly facts; thus the four noble truths are featured as the most important things in your mind. *The Great Discourse* is utterly amazing in the way Buddha leads his disciples through this. After all, his enlightenment under the bodhi tree occurred when he himself became perfectly clear on these four noble truths, especially the third one, the noble truth of freedom from, cessation of, blowing away of, suffering.

So the Buddha leads us patients into the subtlest organization of the mind-objects, that of the four noble truths, or realities. These four things are possibilities for ordinary persons but are realities for a "noble," truly friendly, person: the realities of suffering, its origination, its cessation, and the eightfold path leading to its cessation. He brings the patients into lucid wakefulness of their diagnosis and prognosis.

First comes suffering in all its detail: birth, aging, death, sorrow, lamentation, pain, sadness, distress, meeting the unloved, losing the loved, dissatisfaction. He then runs through the five aggregates again—our body, sensations, perceptions, thoughts, and consciousnesses—this time in brief as suffering processes. He directs us to focus on a list of agreeable and pleasurable things to impress on our awareness how craving for more and better always spoils these impermanent experiences because they do not last; they are the suffering of change.

Next he turns to the origination of suffering, directing mindfulness to pinpoint craving for the agreeable and pleasurable, and again he turns the focus onto the five aggregates. The mindful awareness of these originating processes of suffering becomes the insight that leads to their cessation, the subtlest level of freedom from the suffering—the mindful awareness of the third noble truth opens the door to the reality of freedom from suffering.

Then comes the most interesting, and even shocking, guidance for the patient. The blowing away of suffering comes from the complete fading of the craving:

> "And what, monks, is the noble truth of the cessation of suffering? It is the complete fading away and extinction of this craving, its forsaking and abandonment, liberation from it, detachment from it. And how does this craving come to be abandoned, how does its cessation come about?"

This leads to the biggest shock in the Buddha's guided meditation that helps the patient mendicants realize the reality of their freedom. The question really is "Where is this freedom from suffering? Where is our nirvana?" And the startling answer is:

> "Wherever in the world there is anything agreeable and pleasurable, there its cessation comes about."

He then goes into the same list of the "pleasurable and the agreeable" that he had guided our minds through in describing the noble truth of suffering, the first friendly fact. This time, however, he locates the cessation of the craving and the suffering right there in the same place where craving and suffering had been happening, precisely in the sites of the experience of what is pleasurable and agreeable. He concludes:

> "And that, monks, is called the noble truth of the cessation of suffering."

Why is this so surprising? Remember that this guided meditation, this sutta, this buddha discourse, is from the Pāli, from the Buddha as heard by individual-liberation-seeking persons who consider nirvana as something other than samsara, liberation as something apart from life. Yet the Buddha clearly states that this nirvanic release is *right here in the world*, right in connection with experience. Craving turns such pleasant experiences into the suffering of change, into dissatisfaction. Yet detachment, freedom from craving, enjoys the very same realities that suffering found intolerable as if they indeed, in reality, are nirvana. This subtly forestalls the patients' tendency to associate nirvana with an escape from experience, a state "beyond," outside of the world of suffering. The lesson is that when you clutch the pleasurable and the agreeable, you stifle it by considering it insufficient, never enough, at which point it terminates and you are left miserably longing for more. When you let yourself go into the pleasurable and agreeable, letting it blow you away by not clutching at it but rather by melting into it, it becomes the revelation of the deep nirvanic nature of reality.

Finally, mindfulness is guided to focus on the fourth noble truth, the eightfold path of realism that we have been studying, which leads to the fading of craving and the gaining of nirvanic freedom from suffering though realistic view, realistic motivation, realistic speech, realistic evolution, realistic livelihood, realistic creativity, realistic mindfulness or remembering, and realistic concentration.

To recap, realistic view is knowing the four truths, processes of causation of suffering and cessation of suffering; motivation is nonviolence, free generosity, and non-alienation; speech is honesty, diplomacy, sweetness, and meaningfulness; evolutionary action is non-killing, non-stealing, non-abuse of sexuality; livelihood is ethical living; creativity is clearing the mind of negativity and sustaining the positive; mindfulness is lucid waking awareness of what is, experiencing it fully without craving and worrying; and realistic concentration is moving into expanded embodiment through moving the mind up through the divine abodes of immense love, compassion, joy, and equanimity, the four contemplations that open for the patients their own inner heavenly nature, which then can manifest right here on earth too. I will return to the eighth of the eightfold path in the forthcoming chapter.

The Buddha concludes this discourse, this guided therapeutic meditation, by telling the patients that they can attain the nirvanic cessation of freedom from suffering in either seven years or even seven days. That is really encouraging, though we must remember he is addressing "mendicants," i.e., dropouts from the household life who are given free lunch by the rich and tolerant Indian society to be on permanent retreat, to just focus on learning, thinking, and realizing lucid waking mindfulness all the time except for eating, sleeping, and bathroom functions! We all tend to be a bit more distracted, what with multitasking, working, taking care of family, and diverting ourselves all too easily! So maybe we need something more like forty-nine days.

In another discourse in the universal vehicle context, the bodhisattva Manjushri leads a divine student through a more explicitly self-transcending version of the four focuses of mindfulness:

> Divine being, moreover, when bodhisattvas observe the body and focus mindfulness, they know that the body of the past was unborn. They know that the body of the future is not accessible. And they understand that the present body is similar in essence to grass, trees, walls, rocks, or visual aberrations. When they observe the body, they understand that the nature of the body is non-arising, and so they do not instigate any contemplation that involves notions of the body. Those who do not instigate contemplation will not dwell on any concerns. Free from concerns and with a consciousness that does not dwell, they train in observing the body and focusing mindfulness on it, yet they neither cultivate nor eliminate anything at all.
>
> Having understood that all things are without reality, they observe the body with the understanding that the mind that observes the body is also just like a magical illusion or an echo. With this wisdom they are neither attached to pleasant sensations nor hostile to painful ones, and since they are also not confused with respect to sensations that are neither painful nor pleasant, they are not predisposed to ignorance. When they are no longer transported by sensations, then this is their focus of mindfulness on the observation of sensations.
>
> As they observe and dwell on sensations their minds are not moved by any movement of their sensations about things, and as their minds therefore do not dwell upon anything, they do

not abandon, discard, or relinquish the spirit of enlightenment. This is their focus of mindfulness on the observation of the mind.

With their knowledge of things actualized, they observe things. At that point they are free from mindfulness and contemplation, and so they understand things' intrinsic nature. They no longer entertain any notions, contemplations, views, or entanglements with respect to body, sensations, mind, or things. This is their focus of mindfulness on the observation of things.

The Buddha's Therapeutic Protocol

As we explore the four focuses of mindfulness, it's worth pointing out that the four noble truths are not a religious credo or prescription for conversion but a clear-cut psychotherapeutic protocol for pragmatic, psychosomatic therapy, designed to lead people out of suffering to enjoy the nirvanic reality of the world. It is intended not merely to annihilate them or to cause them to resign themselves to their misery but to bring them to bliss. Freud said his psychotherapy was designed to lead people from neurotic suffering into acceptance of regular suffering, not because he was being stingy with them but because he had no idea that there was such a thing as fully blissful living (although maybe he thought he knew about it when he was high on cocaine, writing some of his great books!). Buddha was way ahead of his time in providing a path beyond suffering altogether.

A Buddhast term for education is *taming*: a giving of tools for taming the psychotic ego, teaching the relative person that she or he is not an absolute entity apart from the world around her or him. This is a far more transformative kind of education or psychotherapy than what we are used to, one that imparts self-awareness and introduces the person to responsibility by focusing their own observation on their relational engagement in the world.

It is not that therapists do not have the goodwill toward their patients to help them become realistic, and even to flourish. It is just that the theory underlying their work makes them feel it is not possible to go further than just achieving a makeshift balance. It has to do with the theory of the unconscious or subconscious. Freud considered the subconscious unknowable by the conscious mind, which is always relegated to being just the tip of the iceberg, inevitably driven by the powerful energies underneath it. The Buddhist scientific view was more thorough, recognizing the situation of the ordinary person as dominated by the powerful subconscious, but also experimentally developing a way for the conscious mind to fully explore the unconscious drives, overcoming delusive misknowings.

Buddha essentially defined enlightenment as becoming fully conscious, free, able to choose the optimal way of being by focusing all energies to be beneficial for oneself and others. This is not a religious matter. It is purely scientific and clinical and arose from genius psychologist self-explorers who became buddhas, wisely and lucidly awake and flourishing persons, who pioneered ways of helping others find their own buddhasmic awakenings. Indeed, in order to do so, these pioneer psychologists had to break away from religions, from their authority and conditioning about the nature of the human and the subjugation of the human being to the caprices of the various gods and their priestly mouthpieces.

Modern psychologists today, who tend to be crippled as Freud was by the dogma of materialism, find it hard to imagine that the buddhist scientists were so far ahead of them in experimentation, discovery of deep psychic realities, and technologies of psychic development, since "modern" is supposed to mean "advanced," and "traditional" thus is supposed to be backward. So they just lump anything remarkable-seeming that was produced by these past sages under the category of "pre-scientific meditation"!

Modern Western Chauvinism Is a Hindrance to Scientific Success

In other words, "Western" chauvinism and "modernist" chauvinism prevent our materialist scientists from learning anything new from the great inner scientists of India and Tibet. The belief has to change that practitioners, whether Buddhist, Hindu, Taoist, or Western mystical, just meditate, defining meditation as learning to be free from thinking, as opposed to defining it as the radical transformation of the most penetrating thinking by experientially discovering the total relativity of the self.

The science-oriented people who do psychology and encounter Buddhism (rarely buddhasm, which is not totally their fault—it's been all too rare!) still cling to the idea that they have the ultimate psychological science, which is necessarily materialist and reductionist, while the Buddhists have meditation but don't really know what they are doing scientifically. These science-oriented people simply think, "Oh, it's just meditation. Amazing! We must figure out how they do it!"

The main problem of the modern Western mind is this: we feel we are the superior people on the planet throughout history. And history is a big deal for us, because it claims to prove that everyone else is more backward than we are. And we are on the frontier of reality, about to find out the quarks, and the gluons, and whatever new things may be discovered. We can actually destroy the planet, and some of us are proud of it. With this belief system comes the notion that we have nothing to learn from anybody in a pre-modern scientific sense. And even though some of us decry and condemn the destructiveness of the direction we are taking, we still feel we are going to reinvent the wheel of how we are going to save ourselves.

The bottom line when it comes to realistic mindfulness or remembering is that the more you learn about reality, the more you have a chance of being free of suffering. That is what the Buddha discovered, and it is not religion. Religion is not defined as coming to an understanding of reality. Actually, science is defined as that, as the attempt to understand reality at its deepest levels. There's a lot more to be said about the Buddhist psychological science, but let's now move on to the top peak of the path, where it all comes together: realistic samadhi, one-pointed super concentration.

CHAPTER 9

Realistic Samadhi

Here we finally come to the summit of the eightfold path, realistic samadhi concentration. We must remember that it is completely connected to the first branch, the realistic worldview of absolute relativity. Without the realistic worldview to provide the aim, any still unrealistic samadhi would only intensify the subconscious core misknowing, meaning that we would end up even more strongly projecting intrinsic reality into everything, especially the deep sense of absolute self-identity. On the other hand, without the realistic samadhi one-pointed concentration, the realistic view would not be able to transform the subconscious unrealistic structures of our misknowing consciousness.

We have learned and analytically meditated enough in this super-education in wisdom on the first two branches of the path, realistic view and realistic motivation.

We have grown to respect the word and so have super-educated ourselves in the ethics of speech and body and made it practical with our livelihood, so our lives are sensibly prioritized and stabilized socially—with realistic speech, evolutionary action, and livelihood.

We have realistically turned our creativity inward into transforming ourselves and so the world, and we have realistically cultivated mindfulness, remembering what is going on in our mind and freeing ourselves from being stuck exclusively in the past or future through memory's endless ruminations and fantasy's anxious anticipations. By now, we are lucidly awake.

But all seven components, though vibrantly activated, have not yet penetrated deep enough within to have transformed the unconscious into our conscious lucid wakefulness, letting us become fully aware of our subconscious and so realize the inner freedom from involuntary reactive drives so we can freely deploy all our formerly repressed energies toward positive accomplishments. We need such freedom to fully transform ourselves into a bliss-being, a buddha, who can lift up the ordinary world itself. This is the power of meditative concentration: when we reside in this state, we are introduced to the freedom that already exists such that we can wake up to bliss. Let's explore what we mean when we talk about "meditation."

Meditation Brings It All to Depth

There are a number of words in Sanskrit that people translate as "meditation," and in English we mainly know about one-pointed meditation from the East and are somewhat aware of critical analytic meditation, as in that of Descartes and so many other great minds.

There is *vipashyana* (the Sanskrit version of the famous Pali *vipassana*), literally a "seeing through," which is analytic meditation that considers things in order to know them realistically.

There is *shamatha*, "serenity," literally "staying in peace," which focuses on one thing and gradually disidentifies with and rules out distracting thoughts and leads the meditator into a state of physical and mental fluency that can be mistaken for the ecstasy of enlightenment.

There is *samāpatti*, total production or immersion, which is best translated as "trance." The Buddha taught a famous set of four entrancements in the formless states: "infinite space," "infinite consciousness," "nothing whatsoever," and "neither just conscious nor just unconscious."

There is *dhyāna* "contemplation" (which resonates through East Asia to us as Chinese *chan*, Korean *son*, and Japanese *zen*), everywhere nowadays in popular culture. It is of course "meditation" or "contemplation," which is the fifth bodhisattva transcendence, and can include both one-pointedness and discursive analysis. There is also a famous set of four contemplations, which are important contents of realistic samadhi: immense love, compassion, joy, and equanimity.

Finally, there is *bhāvana*, which comes from a verb "to be" or "to become" and is often translated as "meditation," but actually might be better translated in some contexts as "realization": to make something real or bring it into being. Thus, when you understand something by reasoning intellectually, that is itself important, but the understanding needs to be brought down from head to heart, needs to be "realized," made real for your whole being.

Climbing Up the Heavens through the Four Immensities

The four immeasurable or immense contemplations—love, compassion, joy, and equanimity—occur when lucid wakefulness brings you into full awareness of the imperfections of the desire realm, so that you renounce the conscious levels of delusion, lust, and hate. You feel so much better in your own skin, hence automatically sympathetic or even empathetic about the condition of others who seem so obviously agitated from within by these impulses they cannot control and must blindly obey. This causes you to feel love for them, not possessive craving but the natural wish for them to be happier, since you have begun to feel happier yourself, having found the cessation of suffering in letting yourself go into the welling up of pleasant sensations in your body and mind.

As long as wakefulness is less than fully stable, you grasp at the slightest emergence of the pleasant, wanting it still more and thereby instantly cutting it off and turning it into an experience of the suffering of change. When it becomes more stable, you are able to let it go on ungrasped, let it flow through you, and so approach the zone of stable happiness known as the love immensity.

The set of the four immense states of love, compassion, joy, and equanimity corresponds to what is referred to as the heavenly realm of desireless form. This realm of subtle, relatively boundaryless embodiment is known to be inhabited by celestial, purely bodied (*brahmakāyika*) deities, "pure" since complete in both male and female gender elements, hence free of desire for the opposite sex, natural celibates. Such pure divine states, however, are not an end goal for you as a bodhisattva seeking buddhahood, though they are important for you to discover and access as part of your discovery of your own inner landscape. Outer cosmos reflects inner landscape.

These immensities are also called the four contemplations (*dhyāna*). The factors enabling these contemplations are attentive consideration, careful analysis, physical fluency, mental bliss, and one-pointed concentration, which are the antidotes, respectively, of the five hindrances: depression, crippling doubt, irritability, agitation, and lust. As you ascend from the full focus of lucid waking mindfulness to the level of feeling the release of inner freedom, you mobilize one-pointedness to launch through the four immensities.

In the first of these four contemplations, that of love, your inner contentment overflows with the feeling of love that surges toward beings who you sense are trapped in frustration and stress, automatically wanting them to feel as happy as you do. You consider other beings' stress compared with your relief, which in turn raises your energy. You analyze how they could be just as happy if they were more realistic. You develop a sense of fluency in your body, and mental bliss arises, making agitation unnecessary. These factors propel your one-pointed concentration into the first zone of immensity, that of immense love that overflows from your own heart toward all other sensitive beings. Though this state is pure flow, its articulation in thought is "May all sentient beings have happiness and the cause of such happiness! Wouldn't it be nice if I could offer that! I must do so!" The flow state is immense and you tend to dwell in it timelessly, and it is appropriately called a "divine abode." When you fully realize it, you become aware that there are numerous divine beings, kind of like angels, who inhabit the same heavenly planes, not as meditating human like yourself but as actual energy embodiments in that immensity. While you admire their

WISDOM *Is* BLISS

loving condition, you restrain yourself from joining them and getting stuck in that state, as you feel the state's remoteness from many levels of being and you seek the buddhahood that interconnects with all.

After some time, as you were previously oriented with motivation to actually bring about your willed happiness, your consideration and analysis functions fulfill themselves by revealing that the beings themselves are not very happy already; they are suffering. Realizing that, your heart gushing immense love moves you naturally into the second of the four, the immensity of compassion. Compassion here is the will to relieve the beings from their suffering and embrace their pains and agonies with the immensity of your flowing loving happiness. Your flow state thus expands even further, leaves behind consideration and analysis, and abides even more fluently and blissfully in the immensity of compassion, articulated in the thought "May all beings be free of suffering and have the causes of freedom from suffering! Wouldn't it be nice if I could offer that! I must do so!"

After a timeless time in the divine abode of the compassion immensity, your sense of constriction within embodiment diminishes naturally. Your physical fluency becomes fulfilled in the immensity of bliss, bliss that overwhelms the perception of constrictedness of beings and resonates with their own inner pleasantness, their own deeper reality of freedom from suffering. At this point you ascend and expand into the third of the four, the bliss of the joy immensity, the factors of consideration, analysis, and fluency all fulfilled in the divine abode of immense joy, articulated in thought as "May all beings have the reality joy that is free of any suffering, and the cause of such joy! Wouldn't it be nice if I could offer that! I must do so!"

Finally, the bliss function becomes fulfilled and you ascend and expand into the fourth immensity, equanimity, wherein you feel a timeless identification with the nirvanic reality of all beings. In this state of equanimity you are close to transcending any sense of separateness of self and others and reach the plane of the divine abode of immense equanimity, where your love, compassion, and joy are completely shared equally with all sensitive life, where your expanded mind is at the plane of the high gods, the Brahmā gods, and this fourth immensity is articulated as the thought "May all beings have the equanimity free of attachment to the dear and hostility to the strange, and the causes of such equanimity! Wouldn't it be nice if I could offer that! I must do so!"

If we use our imagination to consider what it feels like to attain such contemplative divine abodes, we can realize how tempting it must be for a yogi or yogini who reaches there to think that s/he has reached divinity, the highest possible state of a being, liberation, divinity, and experiential oneness with all living beings and things. In fact, a yogi or yogini who is unprepared will definitely consider these abodes as far preferable to ordinary desire-realm humanoid planes or even desire-realm pleasure heavens and would be quite likely to choose rebirth in the court of great Brahmā, or even seek his throne. Alternatively, it is reported that there are four further, more subtle states of disembodiment for the more sensitive and therefore ascetically inclined: the immaterial states or rather mediums (as they go beyond relative spatiality) of infinite space, infinite consciousness, seeming nothing whatsoever, and beyond being either conscious or unconscious. These states may be even more seductive to one who is totally bent on having their own peace and quiet, seemingly permanently, without any disturbance.

As for the divine beings who embody this sense of immensity of the divine form realms, it is said that there are 16 or 17 heavenly planes that are the abodes of numerous pure-bodied deities who have landed there out of attachment to those heavens. Beings in these realms have subtle, semi-boundaryless bodies and use only three senses—sight, hearing, and touch—as they live on pure energy and have no need of taste and smell. I think of them as gigantic energy whales who lack hard boundaries and sexual differentiation and just surge around feeling love, compassion, and joy as they merge in and out of each other. When they reach the seven last levels of equanimity, they verge on infinity, where embodiment seems to vanish in a release free of any sense of loss.

The yogis and yoginis who visit these realms in lucid wakefulness and the deities who have been reborn in these relatively lust-free, pure form realms are androgynous, self-aware, non-coarse-physical bodies of bliss nurtured by pure energy immersion, and the gradations relate to varying degrees of subtlety until, at the top level, the bodies are as close to pure light as can be and still be a body. While these are wonderful states to be in, they are not the pure bliss of nirvana, which is a kind of bliss that simultaneously and inconceivably interfuses with all other life-forms, even the most dense and alienated by misknowing.

Loosening the Self and Relaxing into Immensity

Imagine you have stilled your mind and focused your consciousness on your own reality as modeled by materialist scientists: focusing on how you are composed of molecules, atoms, subatomic particles, waves, and super-subtle, wave-particle-objectively-indeterminate energy phenomena. You focus within to such a degree of subtlety that you experience yourself dissolving into this super-subtle world, yet you remain conscious of yourself as its flowing, super-subtle, fragmented, and fragmenting processes.

It seems inconceivable, of course, as our habitual consciousness seems to conform to our concepts of hard-boundaried self and things, but this is what the yogic progression up through the four immensities seems to consist of. It is truly what may underlie the meaning of the word "sublimation," in that the energies of instinctual lust and conscious desire are restrained and re-channeled back into oneself, and instead of melting outward into another in sexual release, one melts into a stable reality in one's own place as mediated by the normally unconscious autonomic (and automatic) central nervous system.

A key point here is that the immensities are not experienced as another place into which the yogi or yogini enters by crossing its boundary. They are experienced as the uttermost inner essential being of where the yogi or yogini is present, the actual presence of the yogi or yogini. The mind, having felt related to ever more subtle, sublimated levels of embodiment, moves into a sense of disembodiment, which at each level is perceived to have always been its own essence as well as that of all other beings.

The immensity of equanimity brings you to the event horizon of departing completely from any sense of embodiment whatsoever, where your one-pointed concentration turns into a formless trance state of complete dissolution of any sense of mass. You self-experience as the infinite mass of pure light, your infinity of presence rendering your sense of differentiable mass irrelevant. Every differentiated material thing, subjective and objective, seems to disappear into the medium of the experience of infinite space, which is experienced as a still deeper, seemingly more releasing bliss, but in a way beyond bliss as release from stress, as the awareness floats free from any sense of restriction or limitation.

As the mind naturally expands into the infinity of this infinite space, it seems as if the insubstantial mind itself becomes infinite and one sublimates or "subtilizes" and releases yet more deeply and intensely into the realm of infinite consciousness.

The unrelenting, not further releasing bliss of this sense of expansion itself becomes so excruciatingly powerful that any sense of even blissful self-presence itself seems a kind of imprisonment, and one moves through a kind of ego-terror into the experience of the medium of seemingly nothing whatsoever, giving up any sense of presence within the bliss by letting self-presence go completely into an experience of nothingness, a kind of consciously sought unconsciousness.

And finally, the sense of infinite/eternal unconsciousness at the most super-subtle level itself seems somehow limited and exclusive, and one goes to the ultimate level of subtlety into the medium and experience of neither consciousness nor unconsciousness.

The four immensities and the four bodiless trances are themselves called the eight planes of sublimational contemplative achievement, and the yogini or yogi who achieves these experiences for real is considered a master contemplative. Buddha himself is depicted as ranging "up and down" or "in and out" of these eight states during the various versions of his demonstration of corporeal death. His final departure from the body in all accounts, in the *Great Total Nirvana Discourses* (*Mahāparinirvāna Sutras*) in either Sanskrit or Pali, occurs when he is at the event horizon between immense embodiment and disembodiment, between the fourth divine abode contemplation and the first formless trance, giving the hint that his buddha-continuum has both physical and mental dimensions even after leaving his previous buddha-emanation body.

The most important point here, one that may differentiate the Buddhist contemplative phenomenology from those of most other mystical traditions, is the point that Buddha made to all his followers. No one of these eight states and experiences is a "state or experience of nirvana"! Not even the most super-subtle seeming, nondual seeming medium of neither conscious nor unconscious trance is nirvana. It is not liberation. It is not the final release from suffering that is buddhahood. A buddha is definitely a master of all eight states, but not a terminal dweller in any one of them, as none of them is the ultimate reality of all things from which a buddha is by definition never apart. Rather, a buddha is defined as someone who is present in all these states and in all other desire-realm states simultaneously, active everywhere out of compassion for other beings still feeling caught in the trap of suffering.

Buddha allowed his individual vehicle students to imagine that nirvana was just such a state beyond the gross physical reality of the desire realm, and beyond even the more subtle pure form realm divine abodes, beyond even the formless media, and maybe something like a state of seeming total obliteration of presence, a kind of "ninth state" beyond the fourth formless medium. He put them into the paradoxical situation of not equating nirvana with any kind of formless state, yet allowed them to think of it as something other than the relative world that they perceived as pure suffering. He taught the samsara-nirvana duality as the provisional situation for those disciples, though as we saw in the *Great Focus of*

Mindfulness Discourse, he is constantly hinting at the non-duality that is the real solution.

In my opinion, that was because their fixated ego-sense was so strong and so rigidly imagined as their real self apart from relational things that they could only envision release as a glorified projection of their desperate desire to withdraw permanently and escape into this imagined absolute, disconnected self. Once they had done their best at that, he knew they would feel more secure and then intended to appeal to their subtle and refined intelligence to recognize that the seemingly separate absolute could not be absolute, since they had related to it by entering it experientially. This then brought them back into contact with the more challenging quest of maintaining the natural bliss of release while remaining infinitely interconnected with everything, which is defined as the fully awakened condition of nirvana.

Non-dogmatism of Buddha's Inner Science

One Buddhist hermeneutical principle more or less agreed upon by all the great Indic philosophers is that the only teaching of the Buddha that is definitive in meaning is emptiness, voidness, selflessness, nirvana, or freedom, all absolute negations. All descriptions of relative realities are conventional and relative, true or false enough, valid or invalid enough, in specific contexts, but none of them is absolute or definitive, so none of them is dogmatically or absolutely true.

Hence a scientific argument can be made that our present materialist astrophysical "standard model" of the universe or cosmos is true for us in our context, accounting for our present sensory and theoretical experiences— Hubble telescope visions, astronautical explorations, etc., and the mathematical theories derived therefrom. But that standard model is not, and may never be, absolutely true forever, and there may be new models developed by the Einsteins and buddhas of the future. Sci-fi writers may be probing imaginatively toward such new models, with materialist scientists trailing along behind mathematically, moving from experiment to experiment.

I often think it is helpful to our absolutism as directed toward the solar system to recognize that everything in the static model we encounter in planetariums is actually in extremely rapid motion relative to any frame of reference outside it. When we stand at the equator, we are in motion with the rotating earth's surface at 1,000 miles per hour; the planet is in motion around the sun at 67,000 mph; the sun is moving through the galaxy at hundreds of thousands of mph; and the galaxy moves within the nebula at an inconceivable speed, basically ad infinitum. So we and the solar system bodies are not static objects but actually ribbons of matter and energy somehow swooshing through the space-time cosmos at dizzying rates all inter-entangled with other swooshing ribbons. Combine that macro inconceivability in your imagination with attempts to picture our micro constitution by wave-particle-indeterminate quantum entities, and you can experience a "collapse of the picturing function" moment.

Turning to the three realms (desire, pure form, formlessness) of the Buddhist inner scientific cosmos, we can return to the contemplative super-education culmination in samadhi, which involves combining serenity, one-pointed concentration, with critical insight contemplation. When that serenity point focuses on the coarse and fine dimensions of our being in the world, we can go in or up with critical insight penetration through the four immensity contemplations and the four formless trance concentrations, and then return to enjoy being present in sensory ordinary existence, carrying the flow of bliss and serenity that suffuses our being. Once we experience any level of the formless mediums, we leave awareness of the body and the heartbeat, and so depart from any sense of time. When we return into lucid wakeful coarse-body sensory awareness, we then confront the issue of "being in time," having experimentally and experientially verified that time itself is not an absolute; time is also a purely relative dimension, just like mass and space.

Super-Subtle Esoteric Inner Science— Tantric Abhidharma

This brings us to the issue of lifespan and death. And here we turn from the Abhidharma, or Super-Science, of the causal individual and universal vehicles and into the Abhidharma Super-Science of the fruitional, secret and subtle universal vehicle known as the tantric or vajra diamond vehicle. This is where the inner exploration of mind realms gets in detail into the exploration of the death and rebirth and between-state (Sanskrit *antarabhava* or Tibetan *bardo)* processes. These are well codified esoterically in the unexcelled yoga tantras, especially in detail in the *Esoteric Community Tantra* literature. They are also popularly known in Tibet and Mongolia, and nowadays all over the world, through the work known as *The Tibetan Book of the Dead*, a misnomer given by its first translator into English; the actual Tibetan title is *The Great Book of Liberation Upon Hearing in the Between*. It was an ironic mistake, since the central insight of that type of inner science work is that there are no such things as "dead people," since people and other beings don't stay dead but just migrate from lifetime to lifetime, always continuing on through various between states.

There is a lot to be said about this, but here you should focus on the contemplative experience of those yogis and yoginis who, in practicing the perfection stages of the unexcelled yoga tantras, contemplatively explore the experience of lucid dying, lucid navigating the between states, and lucidly taking rebirth. Through samadhic mastery of the subtle levels of mind experienced, they report learning how to remain lucid during these experiences (as in lucid dreaming)—contemplatively rehearsing lucid dying and being lucidly reborn back into their own coarse bodies, without actually dying and having to find rebirth as a new human fetus in a womb.

Most important are the set of eight inner states they report having traversed in the dying process (astonishingly similar to the eight concentrations we have just discussed). To list them in a table:

Eight Stages of Death-Dissolution

Dissolution	Inner Experience
1. Earth to water	Mirage, hallucination
2. Water to fire	Smoky envelopment
3. Fire to wind	Fireflies swirling in sky
4. Wind to consciousness (or space)	Still candle flame
5. Consciousness to luminance	Clear moonlit white sky
6. Luminance to radiance	Clear sunlit red sky
7. Radiance to imminence	Clear pitch-darkness
8. Imminence to clear transparence	Clear twilight predawn gray sky

These eight dissolution stages are developed out of an experiential gradient that no doubt could be divided into a larger or smaller number of levels. It has been regularized

over centuries by the "psychonaut" explorers who have
ventured into the inner realm of this most important time
in the life-and-death process, as most useful for those
seeking to refine their consciousness to include such subtle planes of their own existence in conscious awareness.

During the first four stages, the subtle consciousness
detaches from its entanglement in the coarse elements—
earth, water, fire, and wind—which stand for the abstract
qualities of solidity, cohesion, temperature, and motion,
together making a coarse body possible. It goes along with
a central nervous system that is schematized as a tree-
like structure of a brow-crown-to-perineum-genital-tip
central channel entwined by two channels on right and
left, which form a trunk with five (or seven, etc.) wheel
nexuses at brain, throat, heart, navel, and genital levels,
from which nexuses branch out the symbolic number of
72,000 nerve channels that animate the sensitivities of
the coarse body.

The withdrawal in dying of the subtle consciousness
from the coarse body is described as the gradual movement of drops of neurochemical awareness from the
peripheral nervous system into the central channel, the
drops themselves associated with the essences of semen
and ovum blood (similar to neurotransmitters such as
dopamine, serotonin, oxytocin, and cortisol). The withdrawal of awareness is schematized into the experience of
the first four inner signs, ending in the single still candle
flame experience.

The deeper withdrawal then ensues as the white drops
from the crown and the red drops from the navel, respectively, descend and ascend through the central channel
until they reach the center of the heart wheel. This is
described as the withdrawal of the super-subtle awareness
from the subtle bodymind to the super-subtle bodymind,

a mentally genetic continuum enclosed in the center of the heart wheel from conception to death. The luminance stage is when the white drops descend from the brain wheel to the heart wheel, the radiance stage is when the red drop ascends from the sub-navel to the heart, and the imminence stage is when the two kinds of drops return to the enclosure of the dark bluish super-subtle bodymind whose wave-particle-paradox-embracing, physical-mental-dichotomy-embracing continuum's presence has been there since conception, in the case of a human mammal, in the womb.

This deeper withdrawal consummates when the imminence threshold state gives way to the clearlight transparency state of the super-subtle bodymind, where lucid wakeful awareness "experiences" the transparency twilight state of the clearlight of the free void. This is defined in Buddhist science as the moment of death, since this super-subtle, dark blue mental gene drop is no longer bound by white and red subtle drops in the heart center, and, if the person is not self-aware of their being at this super-subtle level, leaves the body and moves out into the cosmos, driven by unconscious drives like a feather in the wind.

The normal, non-subtle-self-aware person's awareness more or less experiences this as total falling asleep, final fainting, passing out, or losing consciousness and never becomes conscious of their own deepest, boundless, infinitesimal and infinite, lucidly awake reality of the clearlight transparency super-subtle level, and is instructed in the *Great Book of Natural Liberation* to try to identify with the infinite-space-like experience as their deepest self.

The reason that this scientific description of the dying process is so important to anyone anticipating or undergoing the dying transition is that it is important to remain calm and fearless when going through it. This is the time when the final samadhi branch of the noble eightfold path really comes into its own, since its yogic development in life has given the wisdom intelligence the microscope-like focus in time and space to perceive the subtle transformations.

Traditionally, what you are told to do is disidentify from the instinctual urges impinging on your illusory fixed self so as not to be thrashed around by them. This enables you as the dying person to have a far more subtle awareness of the specifics of the process, so as to enter lucidly into the inevitable release of the great bliss of death, the letting go of all stress of boundaries and conflicts of self and other. If you can go through this kind of subtle transition calmly, you have the best chance of migrating consciously into better and better future life situations. Knowing the layout of the experience is thus extremely helpful. Even more helpful, of course, is rehearsing the process in contemplative exercises ahead of time, though obviously you have to be extremely well instructed, highly developed, and even then very cautious and careful.

Living Mindfully in the Face of Death

In living the evolutionary life in the light of inevitable death, having this kind of road map of the death process and wishing to prepare to be able to undergo it with some degree of lucidity are very helpful in trying to live more lucidly.

You can come to see your living process and your contemplative journeys, which you embark upon to discover your more subtle inner dimensions, as a between state, or *bardo,* just as your dream states are. You can begin to live more holistically in the six betweens—the waking life betweens, the dream betweens, the contemplation betweens, the death point betweens, the reality betweens, and the existence or emergence betweens—up to the brink of being conceived in another life.

Awakening, or enlightenment in this context, is to undergo all of them consciously, lucidly, with mindful awakeness, lucidly dreaming, lucidly journeying in contemplations, and of course being lucidly self-directing during the dying and post-death betweens.

For anyone who wants to wake up, there is a great opportunity in this dying process to practice the letting go or giving-away-of-self process and to experience the clearlight transparency state as a stage of liberation. One becomes free to be all that as blissful peace, while also effortlessly navigating specific responses from the super-subtle bodymind continuum to the stressed feelings of other beings who are struggling.

This is the time when samadhi meditation as the empowering force of concentration becomes utterly indispensable. This is where samadhi helps you drill your way to the inconceivable release of buddhahood while not abandoning all the relational beings your innate, selfless super-bliss allows you to love without reservation.

Some might now think of this amazing inner science approach to the dying and rebirthing process as somehow a tantric intrusion developed and refined in Tibet. It is true that the great Tibetan inner scientists, scholar-sage-yogis and yoginis, preserved and hugely developed the study, practice, and achievement of Buddha and his Indian successors' teachings and scientific studies of the tantras. Nevertheless, there is no doubt that this analysis of the death process is drawn from the Indian inner science of Buddha and his enlightened successors.

Take a look at the eight stages of dissolution and the eight coarse mentality contemplative states taught in the

Pali and Sanskrit early sources. To put them side by side in another table:

Eight Stages of Death-Dissolution and Eight Contemplations/Trances

Dissolution	Inner Sign	Contemplative State
I. Earth to water	Mirage	Love immensity
2. To fire	Smoky	Compassion immensity
3. To wind	Fireflies swirling	Joy immensity
4. To consciousness (space)	Candle flame	Equanimity immensity
5. To luminance	Moonlit sky	Infinite space
6. To radiance	Sunlit sky	Infinite consciousness
7. To imminence	Pitch-darkness	Nothingness experience
8. To clearlight transparency	Twilight sky	Neither conscious nor unconscious

The reason I like this comparison so much, and had a really strong "Eureka!" feeling when I first noticed it, is that it proves to me Buddha's honesty when he said to his individual vehicle disciples that he had not withheld any teaching from them. He picked up a handful of leaves and showed them in his hand and said words to the effect of "I have held nothing back in the closed fist of a bad teacher! Though of course, there are also as many teachings in the buddhaverse as there are leaves out there in the forest!" In the inner science cosmology, he was teaching that they had the states of form and formless realms within their experiential reach, and that they would experience them anyway every time they died or even fell asleep! And he was even hinting that they had the buddha-nature already within themselves, an awakening or complete buddha all-knowing awareness already there within, just covered over by a shell of misknowing.

Imagine: Shakyamuni Buddha thus taught the bardo between-state teachings in his earliest contemplative cosmos inner science teachings, and we are all still trying to catch up with them 2,500 years later!

Supernormal Awarenesses and Powers

Speaking of catching up with Buddha, in visiting this amazing samadhi branch of completing the super-education in mind, you have to consider the subject of the supernormal (I never say "supernatural," as these are all quite natural) super-knowledges or super-knowings (*abhijñā, abhiññā*), and superpowers, which include teleportation and telekinetic powers, clairvoyance, clairaudience, former life remembrance, telepathy, and knowledge of the termination of contaminants, or, we can say, nirvanic reflexive awareness.

The inner science says that these super-knowings are natural, the mundane five automatically attainable at the fourth immensity of one-pointed equanimity, and the sixth super-knowledge attainable with the attainment of partial nirvana at sainthood (arhatship) or total nirvana at buddhahood. The mundane five are said to pose the danger of causing distraction on the way to full awakening but are considered useful, even indispensable for an awakened bodhisattva or buddha to make her or his teaching more effective in helping others. I am still hoping that will be the case.

If all this inner science cosmology and even eschatology seems overwhelming, it should be noted that the ultimate super-subtle reality pervades all relative reality, all theories are only useful hypotheses guiding further experience and experiment, and there is no ultimate dogmatically absolute theory of everything. The universe is neither only matter nor only mind, and so considering it reductively one way or another is just a way of guiding experience to realize its mind-matter-nondual inconceivable reality. Therefore, the inner science is delighted to honor and utilize in study and implementation the amazing discoveries of the Western outer, materialistic sciences through the exploration of the macro and micro cosmos, galaxies, and universes, as well as cells, molecules, DNA, RNA, atoms, subatomic quanta, and subparticulate energies. Inner scientific Buddhasts are only asking the outer scientists for the philosophical development and the contemplative achievement of the mental resilience that will enable reciprocity, as the inner scientific discoveries are explored by outer scientists in our current pluralistic age.

So realistic samadhi is when we bring to life all the other seven facets of the jewel of realism, in full liberation, bright awakening, and inconceivable enlightenment itself.

Intellectual Superiority and Buddhism as Realism

It's a big thing for me, in speaking to Western Buddhists, to get them to think about learning something. They are so arrogant about their Western, English-formulating intelligence that they think they have nothing to learn from some ancient culture of a bunch of non-technological people, except maybe how to meditate or not overcook vegetables or something. The idea that they might, in some respects, be intellectually inferior to some ancient people is really hard for them to grasp—really hard!

It's difficult for many people to feel intellectually inferior, regardless of their cultural background . . . the ego jumps in and reasserts itself! But in the present historical moment, there is something we don't know that we have to learn. Otherwise, the backward, materialist, consumerist, and militarist culture we have developed is poised to destroy all human life!

The Tibetan word *nang pa*, from Sanskrit *adhyātmika*, literally means "insider." For centuries it has been the basic word for "a Buddhist." Its most basic definition is someone who has gone inside the three refuges of the jewels of the Buddha, the Dharma, and the Sangha, which can be thought of as the teacher, the teaching and the reality taught, and the society of those seeking that reality. It's like we say in English: you're in the "in group" or not. However, Buddhist scholars in India, as well as Tibet, sometimes say that the inside meant by "insider" refers to an orientation, such as that toward the inner science of the mind, how the mind is bound in egotistical delusion, and how it is liberated through critical wisdom aligned with higher concentration. This is scholarly creativity.

If you take the three refuges as simply meaning denominational belonging, it doesn't sound that great to be an "insider": it definitely is a form of exclusivism. It's like His Holiness the Dalai Lama speaking at Harvard Divinity School's Center for the Study of World Religions, telling people that he didn't believe in God and he wanted them to know it right away, because otherwise they might get to liking him, only to later discover that he didn't believe in God, and at that point they might actually faint! So he wanted them to know right off the bat.

However, if we really think about what the three refuges are (this is kind of important for me), of the three, the real refuge is the second, the Dharma. Vasubandhu said that *dharma* has 11 meanings, the highest of which is reality itself, the only truly real reality being nirvana (the relative realities being slightly less real, luckily). That means that when you take refuge, you are taking refuge in reality itself, which is the only sensible thing to do, since we have to live in reality. And actually, if we give the Buddha some credit, we can embrace reality with some confidence that it is good, it is safe, it is bliss, it is freedom, it is love, and it is compassion.

You take refuge in the Buddha less directly, not as a person who can save you, since he clearly stated that he could not, but as a teacher who pointed out to you after discovering it himself that reality is good, nirvana, freedom from suffering. You also take refuge in the third of the three, the Sangha, indirectly, as those who join you in your refuge in the true reality of nirvana. Taking refuge in reality, of course, is equivalent to being realistic, truly realistic to the bitter end.

To repeat what I often say when asked "What is Buddhism?":

Buddhism is engaged realism.

Just this is what I mean. So "insider" in this case means anyone who does not think that ignorance is bliss, but rather that knowledge, freedom from ignorance, wisdom—these are bliss. A humanistic scientist therefore can qualify as an "insider." A theist who thinks that God must be the highest reality, the supreme truth, perhaps an impersonal force of love and creativity, etc., who may disregard culture-specific tenets about tribal male deities with beards and thunderbolts, who demand unrealistic blind faith—such a person can be considered an "insider."

The Psychonauts: Inner Science Astronauts

Tibetan inner scientists certainly concern themselves much more with the inner universe than the outer one. I have called their adepts "psychonauts," or mind explorers, in parallel with the heroes of Western science, the "astronauts," who explore the stars, the farthest frontiers of the material macroverse. These psychonauts maintained and developed the esoteric traditions known as tantra, which constitute the super-subtle science and technology of the universal vehicle adepts. As their science was quint-essentially an "inner science," using the human brain and body and the out-of-body subtle body subjectivity as the laboratory, these adepts also developed an inner technology. Then, because they were lucidly awake in life, they were able to lucidly dream, lucidly sleep, lucidly wake, lucidly live, lucidly die, and lucidly create new embodiments—at full buddhahood, even multiple embod-iments simultaneously.

The Tibetan view is that these psychonauts are there-fore consciously immortal, like true Jedi masters, and they remain with beings—not just beings on this planet, not just humans, and not just Buddhists, but all sentient beings—because their indefatigable dedication is to help all beings evolve and find their own liberation from suf-fering. Though none of them is omniscient or omnipotent in a quantitative sense theoretically, a being that becomes self-identified with an infinite relativity should be able to marshal knowledge and competency from other areas and eras of such infinite relativity to bring to bear a virtually absolute accuracy on any particular relational situation, assisting sensitive beings in evolving toward freedom from suffering. This sense of the ultimately overwhelming power of the good guys and the good gals explains the remarkable resilience of Tibetans such as the Dalai Lama, the other developed lamas, and the ordinary Tibetan people living in their aura in the face of the horrendous ordeals they have undergone since being invaded by the Chinese People's Liberation Army in 1950.

Although they do not believe in the coherence of the idea of an omnipotent God who created the world, controls all things in the world, cares for them, and yet leaves them filled with difficulties for some inscrutable reason, their sense of the infinite relativity of a beginningless and end-less universe causes them to side with the probability that, given infinite and beginningless and endless opportunity, infinite numbers of beings must have become relatively more powerful on the side of goodness, joy, love, gentle-ness, and even fun. Therefore there is no limit to what goodness, truth, and beauty they can eventually mani-fest, discover, realize, and create, and this really excellent buddhaverse is open to be as great as they can make it, sooner or later.

There is a form of fully awakened Buddha called a "Time Machine" (*Kālachakra*), who is ultra-esoteric, a manifestation of the buddhas that demonstrates their unfailing cosmic engagement in the destiny of all sen-tient beings. It is the most advanced Buddhist theory of history, and is the place where Buddhism becomes most graphically buddhasm! It reveals that under the guidance of the omnicompetent buddhas, we live in a buddhaverse, not a universe, and that buddhaverse is, *pace* Voltaire, "the best of all possible worlds." It is an ideal evolutionary space-time, ideal for the acceleration of the evolution of all sentient beings toward the supreme form of life, the buddha life, the life of a being who is all love and all wis-dom, finally perfectly adapted to absolute relativity by fully identifying with all other beings. Again, this is not a matter requiring religious belief; rather, it is an invitation to take advantage of the evolutionary opportunity.

It connects with the prophecy of the advent of the ideal land of Shambhala, an egalitarian-in-principle con-stitutional monarchy, wherein everyone, female and male, old and young, is oriented toward the maximization of meaningful evolution. It is mysteriously hidden from the misknowledge-dominated land of struggle, of war, holocausts, plagues, famines, and death-ridden subsistence life. But it will emerge in a few centuries in a planetary restoration, after the scourges of consumerism and militarism have run their course. However, there is no need to wait for that to happen. Anyone who discovers the perfection and beauty of this world of evolutionary opportunity, even in the midst of the struggles of today, can turn their steps in this most positive of directions and live the "new age" from day one. This is the key to the happiness and joy we can implement from within, on our own way to becoming buddhas.

CHAPTER 10

Sharing My Consolation Prize

Well then, we have gone through the entirety of the Four Noble Truths, or as I call them, the four friendly facts.

The first of the four was the diagnosis. Buddha says if you're not enlightened, that means you don't know what you are, and you don't know what the world you're in is really about. Therefore, you're going to have a frustrating time, because you're going to be wandering like a blind person on the freeway. That's not even a genius statement; it's an obvious statement. If you don't know what's going on, you're going to have a hard time.

It's very simple, although he said it's a fact for a noble, truly friendly person. He had a special definition of noble. "Noble" means someone who has a degree of altruistic perception, not just a moralistic attitude about altruism, and who therefore perceives the life pulse of others as equal to their own in importance and in reality, and who therefore is truly friendly with other beings.

The second truth stems from the fact that most people are not going to agree that ordinary life is suffering. They have moments of relief; they have moments of pleasure and pain. It's not all suffering, so they won't agree with that, so it's not a fact for them.

This second truth is that there's a cause of that unenlightenment. What's the cause? The cause is self-centeredness. Not that people are immoral; it isn't that. They can be quite moral by following rules. It's that the unenlightened person thinks, *I'm the one!* like Neo in *The Matrix*. Many of us here might be thinking that. Each person is the main person in their own life, right? Don't we think that? At least we think we're supposed to look out for number one, be responsible, whatever. We make ourselves separate from others, and we crave for things to be a certain way, and this separates us further into an unrealistic state of alienation because we quickly notice that other people don't normally think we're the one— except maybe Mom or Dad or maybe, perhaps temporarily, someone who is in love with us.

Then Buddha gave a very hopeful and very surprising prognosis: the third noble truth. Nobody believes it, really. It's the prognosis that you can be free of suffering— really free of suffering, not just enjoying temporary relief, a bit of pleasure that won't last from some external event or some success or the acquisition of something or a nice relationship. But that just from within, from knowing your own true nature, you can have perfect freedom from suffering. He taught that, and he manifested it himself, and many people realized it in his own time. Subsequently many people have realized that, and probably some of you have realized it.

The prognosis is very, very good. You're taught, in our somewhat constricted culture and somewhat militaristic society, coming from a Euro-American colonialist past, that you're hardwired and there's nothing you can do about it. The way the Buddhist inner scientists understand your humanity, however, is that you are not very hardwired at all.

The Buddhist view is that the human being is completely malleable in their wiring. Any human being can become a saint and very easygoing, and any human being can become quite evil and very, very difficult, if they go on the dark side, and all degrees in between. Actually, every human being is constantly changing all the time. If you don't become more conscious about how you change and what changes things and what influences you, and you do not choose what you allow to influence you by using your intelligent discrimination, then you will probably be changed for the worse.

This is why we have the fourth truth and that's the eightfold path. The eightfold path is like a whole curriculum of a university. It should be the core curriculum of all our liberal educating universities, 100 percent.

The first path asks, What is real versus what is unreal? This is what we referred to as realistic worldview. Are you just a brain being carried around on top of a skeleton, in between Halloweens, rattling around in there, hopefully producing a lot of dopamine to make you feel better without any malevolent drugs? Hopefully that's what you are, but are you that? Are you merely a brain? Is your life really meaningless, ultimately? Does nobody really care about it? Should you therefore, realistically speaking, not really care about it, except for what you can get out of this or that pleasure? Do you have a purpose? How happy can you be?

Even that's open to question. I think most people don't think they can really be that happy. They feel wisdom is a kind of resignation to carrying your misery with nobility. Just stagger around and have the occasional glass of wine. Even the idea of nirvana, that you can be perfectly happy—sure, give me a break.

That's why Buddha was so smart. For less capable people, he was careful not to really say nirvana is bliss. He would just say that nirvana is freedom from suffering; it's the end of suffering. He didn't really say bliss that much—now and then, but not all the time. He just said end of suffering and let people think about what that might be, probably knowing that the more psycho among them would just think it was an annihilation, anesthesia, you know. That was more sensible to them. They would be less skeptical about that.

Your realistic worldview is that you're here forever, and you have to be concerned not just with your old age and your pension; you have to be concerned with your next life. The way to be concerned for your next life is to invest now in your mind and get your mind open and clear.

That's the first thing: once you have that realistic worldview, you realize you are a precious continuum of good energy, still dragging along behind you some bad energy, and your job as a human is to take this unique opportunity to really increase the good exponentially, and really decrease the bad just as exponentially.

Then you have the realistic motivation. (Sometimes people like to translate it as intention; I like motivation.) So realistic motivation: once you have adopted compassionate commitment to causality, then your motivation is to associate yourself with all good causes and reduce connection to negative causes. You are an evolving being, and you should develop the motivation to use your time of being conscious so that you're motivated to always choose the positive, even if it's the tiniest little thing. And your motivation is to always choose the slight increment that's better as opposed to the increment that's worse.

Then, from realistic motivation, realistic speech is next. Speech should be only truthful, it should be only peacemaking, it should be only gentle, and it should be only meaningful. Babbling meaninglessly, or harshly, or untruthfully, or making people enemies with each other, thinking that you'll get a benefit out of that: those kinds of speech are really negative actions, and sadly very powerful.

Next you have what's called realistic evolutionary action. Realistic karma doesn't just mean any act; it means an evolutionary act, an act you do with a certain intention. Because your mind is involved, it will change the shape of your life. What you do changes the way you are, and not just what you do physically. What you do verbally and what you do mentally will change the mode of your life. You want to do only that which will change your life and your mind for the better. What you discover with realistic evolutionary action is that the mind causes change, and therefore you have to gain leverage over your mind.

You might think, *Somebody was mean to me,* and then you brood and brood, and then you can't get out of that cycle of brooding, which will lead to being depressed and freaked out. Instead, you feel there is a part of your mind that is brooding, and you tell it, *I'm not going to listen to you anymore. They were unpleasant yesterday but forget them. I'm going to have a happy time today; I'm going to do something else.* You can switch.

As I said before, it's like you get a clicker for your mind. Otherwise you have to follow everywhere your mind leads you; you're just a victim of thoughts that are put in there by conditioning, that you have no control over, so you're just a victim of your environment and you don't have any freedom in your mind. When your mind tells you, *Oh, he said that to me, I have to get freaked out,* can you instead sit back and say something else? *Why should I do that? What good is that going to do? That's not going to help.* Your more intelligent mind comes and intervenes, and you have a dialogue inside yourself. That's not a sign of dementia; that's a sign of waking up.

Then there is realistic livelihood, number five. You shouldn't have a profession where you're doing something harmful to anybody. You shouldn't work for companies that do harmful things to people. You should only have a livelihood that benefits people, because you get an evolutionary impact from it. That's very important. The professions of weapons makers, butchers, alcohol distributors, and addictive drug pushers of various kinds are all strongly disrecommended. You can figure that out for yourself. That's realistic livelihood.

Then six is realistic creativity. This is where you get out of your laziness. You become really creative when you realize that you have to do something about your life in your mind, that no one else can do it for you. I love that about Buddha. Buddha's like, "Oh wow, I'm enlightened, I'm so cool. I now am happy because I see you can become enlightened, but I can't make you enlightened. You have to understand your own state. You can do that, I see that, but you have to do it yourself. I can't understand yourself for you. You have to understand yourself. Faith alone will not make you enlightened. Understanding makes you enlightened, and you have to have that understanding."

That's why Buddha's big job was to found a school—really not a religion, but a school. It's not just a school to enable you to have a profession and produce things, it's a school to make you evolve. You produce yourself in a future world, and you are able to do things for other beings and produce their happiness by being a loving being in both this and a future world. That's what it's about: to really be, competently, a loving being. That's quite a task, and that's what you become when you become enlightened.

Then there's realistic mindfulness. After creativity, mindfulness. Mindfulness really means becoming self-aware in a different way. It doesn't just mean when you're meditating; it also means to be more self-conscious of yourself when you're interacting with people. The groundwork of it is counting one to ten, counting your breath, looking there at yourself. The real groundwork is to become aware, to observe how your mind works inside and how your thoughts link together. And you find the gaps in those links and learn to interfere with the ones that are going in the wrong direction and to empower the ones that are going in the right direction. At first you just want to see what's happening. That's realistic mindfulness.

Finally, the last of them all is the true meditation one, which is realistic samadhi, a concentrated, one-pointed meditation. In other words, you shouldn't do heavy meditation, really intense, shutting your mind onto one point, until you know which point to shut it down on. If you take your ignorance and become concentrated on it, you will become more magnificently ignorant. That's really very important, as there's a lot to learn.

As I mentioned, Buddhism is like a school, and it has many courses. They're open to all to take. You don't have to be Buddhist, and you don't have to become Buddhist either. You'll be a better Christian, or Jew, or secularist, or whatever you will, if you study from those courses. Of course, Buddhists should study other courses. The Dalai Lama's always sending his monks off to Christian monasteries and convents to study how those monks and nuns do this and that. He particularly likes the Catholic nuns who run hospitals and do other good works. He thinks the Buddhists don't do enough of that, and he likes that very, very much.

So that's the eightfold path, and that was Buddha's basic therapy. It was Buddha's basic force for good, his vision for the world, like his education system. What you see the Dalai Lama doing is not promoting Buddhism; he may do that for Buddhists, but for others he's not promoting any such thing. He is trying to change the education system to bring more compassion and love into people's minds as part of their education. And of course, the root of compassion is realistic wisdom: knowing what reality is. The more you know what reality is, the more you know you really do depend on others. And then you know the quality of your life depends to a huge degree on your relationships with others. Therefore you will find the resources for the inner bliss that enables you to be more loving and compassionate to others. And then you'll be happy.

Sharing My Consolation Prize

Nowadays when I share some teachings with students, the question comes up, I guess at the beginning as well as at the end: Where do I myself stand? Am I "enlightened" myself, and speaking from "there" as I tell them about all these buddhas and bodhisattvas, about the infinite lifestyle, bliss, buddhahood, the positive, glorious, exquisite nature of reality? Or am I just doing wishful thinking, rationalization, living in fantasyland?

I always honestly answer, "No, I am not enlightened! I am just like you, looking for it, hoping for it!" I sometimes say, jokingly to lighten things up, "Actually I want to reassure you that I am actually quite miserable, just as honorably miserable as many of you may be, though I hope a bit less after our conversations these days!" There is often a sigh of disappointment when I speak like this, in one way, and maybe a feeling of relief in another.

My wife scolded me recently about how I always intensively deny how I'm enlightened—which I do, especially around the house, or I'm in real trouble. She said, "Yeah, that's correct. You're an idiot. But in a way you are more enlightened than most people, so it would discourage them too much if you keep insisting on how unenlightened you are. So shut up and admit to a bit of enlightenment."

Of course I am not a buddha, since I cannot hold my mind on a dot of blue color for two hours without wavering, I cannot levitate, I cannot wakingly emerge in a subtle body out of my coarse ordinary body, I cannot fly through the air, I cannot live in a 20-below mountain winter stark naked, I cannot conjure jewel trees out of toothpicks, radiate light rays from my forehead, I cannot talk to the gods, ward off demons, heal my friends, calm my enemies. I cannot liberate Tibet and all prisoners of conscience and all victims of famine, genocide, war, and disease all over the world. I cannot find souls in the between states and move them into buddhaverses. I cannot even be sure my teachings have any positive effect on my students.

I definitely believe the buddhas and advanced bodhisattvas can do such things. But after more than half a century of study and practice, I have failed at any of the above attainments, and I must admit I am still a tiny bit unsure whether my belief in them is correct or mistaken.

I did, however, succeed in awarding myself a consolation prize to console me in my failure. It came to me one day when I was looking at some family photos in a scrapbook. I came upon a picture of myself and my beloved wife, partner, and teacher, Nena, with our first two children on the beach in the island of Majorca when we were 29 years old. It was a sunny little bit of paradise, immensely enjoyable to see as a pic and to remember. But then my enjoyment was disturbed when I looked at my own face, and in a flash recognized the thought in my mind at the time, which was a strong sense of anxiety in the midst of the blissful scene. "Where is the wallet, the credit card? Are we almost out of money? Where is my visa for India, where a fellowship awaits? Are the kids okay? Is Nena happy? What do we need?" Et cetera. I could see from the picture that I was not "in the moment," realistically aware of the blessed fortune, blissful setting and companionship, and peaceful situation on a planet where many beings were suffering, dying, starving, feeling sick, in agony, terrified, tortured, and so on.

But then I realized that I now could see how wonderful the situation was, how lucky we were, how blissful and blessed with fortune. I enjoyed the scene immensely, even blissfully, *retroactively*, in that way.

I then realized something about the nirvana reality that Buddha discovered and proclaimed to our world in this era. This nirvana reality is not a created state. Not a new place created by causes, by effort. It is the ultimate, "Oh, I knew that all along. How come I didn't recognize it before now? It has obviously always been that way!"

If nirvana is there at all, it has to have always been there, or *here*, from beginningless time. And when it is experienced as the reality home it has always been, all of one's past experiences are reexperienced as having never been apart from that nirvana. I suddenly then realized how it was that the Buddha could experience all his infinite previous lifetimes just at the brink, the event horizon, of realizing the beginningless, eternal reality of nirvana. He had forgotten so many of those lives because he had experienced them as suffering, as painful, and who wants to remember pain? No one wants to feel pain, and after having done so, no one wants to remember having felt it. But if you realize that you have always *really* been in nirvana, then you see your past painful experiences as illusory reflections in the bliss-polished mirror surface of unwavering bliss, freedom from any pain. They are not 100 percent nonexistent; they were experienced as painful due to your failure to know their deeper nirvanic reality of inconceivable graceful bliss. And since you then can see without diminishing the presence of such overwhelming super-bliss throughout all your limitless infinite previous lives, you can also see your beginningless and endless entanglement with the infinite pasts of all the countless other beings without exception, all of whom, unbeknownst to too many of them, have also never been apart from the uncreated inconceivable bliss of nirvana.

No one is left out, and it becomes totally natural for you to want everyone else to know their own reality. You can even see how they inevitably will do so, given infinite time to eventually overcome their misknowing, given the infinite numbers of beings who have already become buddhas and only wish them to do so, and given that these buddhas have the power and the artfulness to effectively help them do so.

So this is my consolation prize. I am not that happy and satisfied and blissful now, but my sense of being isolated in a "now" moment cannot withstand analysis. I have no good reason to not believe I am engaged in endless continuity; and I have good reason to believe the Buddha, because he knew and taught the emptiness and relativity that I can experimentally and experientially verify. So I can be profoundly certain that I will also become such a buddha, experience such a nirvana, and join the buddha and bodhisattva team to effortlessly bring other beings into their own blissful awareness of being in that beginningless flow of bliss and love.

This is my consolation. This very moment here and now will be known *later* as already experienced here and now as bliss-void-indivisible, super-bliss-freedom-inseparable, totally indivisible universal communion of all individuals, *retroactively*. Not only this moment here and now, fleeting as it is, but all the infinite past moments of all the experiences of all my existences and all those of all my fellow beings will be revised in the light of every single one's, yours as well as mine, nirvanic freedom and will be thoroughly known as pure bliss, not only forever after, but forever *before*. The past also will be transformed and all tragedies rectified and immersed in blissful happiness.

This is the consolation prize I have awarded myself and am utterly delighted to share with you.

This is why I'm happy to share that buddhas have more fun. You might think that once you are immersed in super-bliss it's boring, that the nature of "fun" is its quality of contrast with boredom, that pleasure must come from its quality of being relief from pain. If there is no pain, there cannot be pleasure. So no fun for buddhas, only boredom. But this is yet another mistake. The point is that buddhas are not alone. No one is ever alone, so why should buddhas be? There are other buddhas, and there are those who do not know they can be buddhas. You have become a buddha yourself through your being blown away in super-bliss—no more pain for you! So you have no more interest in your own condition; you have completely *gotten over yourself.* Yes, you are bored, but only with yourself! Your awareness of others has become unlimited, and for you they are the most interesting parts of your infinite self. And your super-bliss energy is like a great wave that lifts them out of their pains, you just have to carefully monitor it not to swamp them. Your fun therefore is their fun, their relief from all pains. And there are always more of them, since they are numberless in the infinite relativity of which you have become blissfully aware. So as a buddha you have more fun than you ever did have, ever could have all alone, with the inexhaustible bliss energy of your love for ever more others, whose immersion in happiness becomes your endless fun!

So, ahaa! A-la-la! Buddhas *do* have more fun! La-la-hoḥ! Settled! A-i-āḥ! And sealed! A-ra-li-hoḥ!

May you feel relieved and blessed by this fact just as much or surely even more than I am! And may such bliss be felt as soon as humanly possible in our indestructible buddhaverse that we all together enjoy and share with each other in wisdom, bliss, and love!

Further Reading

Dalai Lama XIV, *Ethics for the New Millennium*. New York: Riverhead Books, 1999.

Dalai Lama XIV, *Freedom in Exile: The Autobiography of the Dalai Lama*. New York: HarperPerennial, 2008.

Dalai Lama XIV, *The Universe in a Single Atom: The Convergence of Science and Spirituality*. New York: Harmony, 2006.

Dalai Lama XIV and Thubten Chodron, *Library of Wisdom and Compassion*. Somerville, MA: Wisdom Publications, 2020.

Jinpa, Thupten. *Tsongkhapa: A Buddha in the Land of Snows*. Boulder, CO: Shambhala, 2019.

Jinpa, Thupten tr. *Essential Mind Training*. Somerville, MA: Wisdom Publications, 2011.

Choden Rinpoche. *Mastering Meditation: Essentials on Calm Abiding and Mahamudra*. Somerville, MA: Wisdom Publications, 2020.

Patrul Rinpoche, Jay L. Garfield tr., and Emily McRae, *The Essential Jewel of Holy Practice*. Somerville, MA: Wisdom Publications, 2017.

Shantideva, and Stephen Batchelor tr. *The Bodhisattva's Way of Life*. Himachal Pradesh: Library of Tibetan Works and Archives, 1999.

Garfield, Jay L. *Engaging Buddhism: Why it Matters to Philosophy*. Oxford: Oxford University Press, 2015.

Thurman, Robert. *Central Philosophy of Tibet*. Princeton: Princeton University Press, 1991.

Thurman, Robert. *Essential Tibetan Buddhism*. New York: HarperCollins, 1996.

Thurman, Robert. *Inner Revolution*. New York: Riverhead Books, 1996. (also audio version)

Thurman, Robert. *Infinite Life*. New York: Riverhead Books, 2005. (also audio version)

Thurman, Robert. *Why the Dalai Lama Matters: His Act of Truth as the Solution for China, Tibet, and the World*. New York: Atria Books/Beyond Words, 2008.

Thurman, Robert. *The Tibetan Book of the Dead: The Great Book of Natural Liberation through Understanding in the Between*. New York: Bantam, 1993. (also audio version)

Thurman, Robert. *Liberation Upon Hearing in the Between*. Louisville, CO: Sounds True Audio, 2005.

Thurman, Robert. *The Jewel Tree of Tibet: The Enlightenment Engine of Tibetan Buddhism*. New York: Atria Books, 2006. Louisville, CO: Sounds True Audio, 2006.

Thurman, Robert. *Indian and Tibetan River of Buddhism*. EdX Online Course, 2019.

Rhie, Marilyn, and Robert Thurman. *Wisdom and Compassion: The Sacred Art of Tibet*. New York: Abrams, 1991.

Armstrong, Karen. *Twelve Steps to a Compassionate Life*. New York: Anchor Books, 2011.

Dyer, Wayne, *The Power of Awakening: The Mindfulness Practices and Spiritual Tools to Transform Your Life*. Carlsbad, CA: Hay House, 2020.

Schell, Jonathan, *The Unconquerable World: Power, Nonviolence, and the Will of the People*. New York: Metropolitan Books, 2003.

Carroll, James, *Constantine's Sword: The Church and the Jews*. Boston, MA: Houghton Mifflin, 2002.

Cahill, Thomas, *Hinges of History* (Six book Series). New York: Anchor, 2006–2014.

Further Reading

William, Anthony, *Medical Medium: Secrets Behind Chronic and Mystery Illness and How to Finally Heal*. Carlsbad, CA: Hay House, 2021.

Hyman, Dr. Mark, *Food Fix: How to Save Our Health, Our Economy, Our Communities, and Our Planet—One Bite at a Time*. New York: Little Brown Spark, 2020.

Greider, William, *One World, Ready or Not: The Manic Logic of Global Capitalism*. New York: Simon & Schuster, 1998.

Iyer, Pico. *The Open Road: The Global Journey of the Fourteenth Dalai Lama*. New York: Knopf, 2008.

Treasury of the Buddhist Sciences American Institute of Buddhist Studies and Wisdom Publications

Jamspal, Lozang, tr. *The Range of the Bodhisattva: A Mahāyānā Sūtra*. New York, American Institute of Buddhist Studies, 2010.

Landesman, Susan A. tr. *The Tārā Tantra: Tārā's Fundamental Ritual Text (Tārā-mūla-kalpa)*. Part I: The Root Tantra. Somerville, MA: Wisdom Publications, 2020.

Chandrakirti, Great Vajradhara, and Robert Thurman, tr. *The Esoteric Community Tantra with The Illuminating Lamp*. Volume I: Chapters 1–12. Somerville, MA: Wisdom Publications, 2021

Kittay, David R. Komodo, tr. *The Vajra Rosary Tantra (Śrī Vajramālā Tantra) by Vajradhara, with Commentary by Alaṁkakalasha*. Somerville, MA: Wisdom Publications, 2020.

Āryadeva, and Christian K. Wedemeyer tr. *The Lamp for Integrating the Practices (Caryāmelāpakapradīpa): The Gradual Path of Vajrayāna Buddhism*. Somerville, MA: Wisdom Publications, 2021.

Khapa, Tsong, and Robert Thurman, tr. *Brilliantly Illuminating Lamp of the Five Stages; Practical Instructions in the Glorious Esoteric Community*. Somerville, MA: Wisdom Publications, 2019.

Wallace, Vesna, tr. *Kālacakratantra: The Chapter on the Individual, Together with the Vimalaprabhā*. New York: American Institute of Buddhist Studies, 2004.

Wallace, Vesna, tr. *Kālacakratantra: The Chapter on the Sādhana, Together with the Vimalaprabhā*. New York: American Institute of Buddhist Studies, 2011.

Gray, David B., tr. *The Cakrasamvara Tantra (The Discourse of Śrī Heruka; Śrīherukābhidhāna): A Study and Annotated Translation.* Somerville, MA: Wisdom Publications, 2019.

Drakpa, Tsong Khapa Losang, and David B. Gray, tr. *Illumination of the Hidden Meaning, Part I: Maṇḍala, Mantra, and the Cult of the Yoginīs.* Somerville, MA: Wisdom Publications, 2017.

Drakpa, Tsong Khapa Losang, and David B. Gray, tr. *Illumination of the Hidden Meaning, Part II: Yogic Vows, Conduct, and Ritual Praxis.* Somerville, MA: Wisdom Publications, 2019.

Drakpa, Tsong Khapa Losang, and Thomas F. Yarnall, tr. *Great Treatise on the Stages of Mantra, Chapters XI–XII, The Creation Stage.* New York: American Institute of Buddhist Studies, 2013.

Nāgārjuna, and Joseph Loizzo, tr. *Nāgārjuna's Reason Sixty with Chandrakīrti's Reason Sixty Commentary.* New York: American Institute of Buddhist Studies, 2007.

Nāgārjuna, and Jan Westerhoff, tr. *Crushing the Categories (Vaidalyaprakaraṇa).* Somerville, MA: Wisdom Publications, 2018.

Buddhapālita and Ian James Coughlan, tr. *Buddhapālita's Commentary on Nāgārjuna's Middle Way (Buddhapālita-Mūlamadhyamaka-Vṛtti).* Somerville, MA: Wisdom Publications, 2021

Maitreyanātha/Āryāsaṅga, Vasubandhu, Lozang Jamspal, tr. and Robert Thurman, tr., et al. *The Universal Vehicle Discourse Literature, together with its Commentary by Vasubandhu.* New York: American Institute of Buddhist Studies, 2004.

Maitreyanātha/Āryāsaṅga and Bo Jiang, tr. *The Sublime Continuum Super-Commentary, by Gyaltsab Darma Rinchen; with The Sublime Continuum Treatise Commentary.* New York: American Institute of Buddhist Studies, 2017.

Madhyāntavibhāga and Mario D'Amato, tr. *Maitreya's Distinguishing the Middle from the Extremes, Along with Vasubandhu's Commentary.* New York: American Institute of Buddhist Studies, 2012.

Saraha and Lara Braitstein, tr. *The Adamantine Songs (Vajragīti).* New York: Columbia University Press, 2015.

Tibet House US—Treasures of Tibet Series

Available from Hay House International (HHI) and Tibet House US (THUS)

Dalai Lama XIV, Sofia Stril-Rever and Sebastian Houssiaux, tr. *My Appeal to the World: In Quest of Truth and Justice on Behalf of the Tibetan People, 1961–2011.* New York: Tibet House US, 2015. (HHI)

Pema Lodoe and Robert Warren Clark, tr. *Dreams and Truths from the Ocean of Mind: Memoirs of Pema Lodoe, the Sixth Sogan Tulku of Tibet.* New York: Tibet House US, 2019. (HHI)

Thondup, Paljor, Douglas Preston and Susan Sutliff Brown. *Undefeated: Confessions of a Tibetan Warrior.* New York: Tibet House US, 2020. (HHI)

Negi, Meenākshī and Robert Thurman, tr. *Mystical Mountains, Rivers of Blood.* New York: Tibet House US, 2017.

Burbank, Michael G., Robert Thurman, and William Meyers. *Man of Peace: The Illustrated Life Story of the Dalai Lama.* New York: Tibet House US, 2017. (HHI)

Rinpoche XI, Lelung Tulki and Tenzin Dorjee, tr. *A Drop from the Marvelous Ocean of History: The Lineage of Lelung Pema Zhepai Dorje, One of the Three Principal Reincarnations of Tibet.* New York: Tibet House US, 2013.

Bultrini, Raimondo and Maria Simmons, tr. *The Dalai Lama and the King Demon: Tracking a Triple Murder Mystery through the Mists of Time.* New York: Tibet House US, 2013.

Dalai Lama XIV. "The Blade Wheel of Mind Transformation by Dharmarakṣita: A Teaching by His Holiness the Dalai Lama XIV." Speech, New York City, September 23–25, 2006. New York: Tibet House US, 2006.

Kistler, Brian, and Robert Thurman. *Visions of Tibet: Outer, Inner, Secret.* New York: Overlook Press, 2006.

Index

S

Acknowledgments

There are so many people I have to thank just for my being here, being able even to write these words to express my gratitude for everything—the best thanks I can think of is to offer this book, this path, this encouragement of everyone who is just like me in having grown up in this world at this time to love the universe, to embrace its deepest reality with total fullness of heart and mind and body and spirit, and not to give up until you have realized that it/he/she/they totally love you back, care for you through life and death and birth and more life, and sing to you, "It's alright already, already and alrighty!"

However, for this book in particular, that it has reached you now at this moment, who may be holding it in your hands or on your screen or listening to it, whoever you may be, I am delighted to single out the incomparable Ms. Patty Gift, Vice President of Hay House International, my dear friend and mentor of some good years by now; her colleague Anne Barthel, another kind person and great Hay House editor; and of course the late Louise Hay, the head man, Reid Tracy, and all the whole team at HHI! Without them this never would have gotten done, and though I am responsible for any faults, they are responsible for any virtues and joys it may be able to awaken in you, dear reader, now and in your future!

Of course, on this day of my 80th birthday, my joyous gratitude for my well-being and inspiration goes always to my late but celestially present dear mother, Betsy, and my dear father, Beverly, and my also beloved spiritual root lama, Venerable Geshe Ngawang Wangyal, whom I only mention for this special purpose in amazed gratitude for the enlightening beginner bodhisattva second birth he awakened in me, as well as my long-lost brothers, David and John, and my niece Myoshin and her lovely partner and children; my continuingly present and endlessly long-living core Lama, His Holiness Tenzin Gyatso, the Great Fourteenth Dalai Lama of Tibet and his whole voluntary-duty planet of 7 billion human brothers and sisters; my beloved ex, Christophe, and all her family, especially our miraculous daughter, Taya, our grandchildren, the late Dash and the thriving Caroline and Max, and Dash's sparkling daughter, our great-granddaughter Secret, with her mother; my day-to-day, indispensable, Guru Angel of Mercy Enlightening Woman Patient and Persevering Mentor, Nena, beloved best friend, our four miracle bodhisattva children, Ganden, Uma (with her lovely hovering ex's), Dechen, and Mipam with sweet Hanna, and our four grandchildren, Maya, Levon, Luna, and Delphine; and to all our great friends, especially late magnificent soul-sister Bobo Bokhara, the great happy-to-be Anonymous Allies all over the country and the world, and those at Tibet House US and at Menla, at Columbia University, and all my graduated students over the decades and their families.

We are all so lucky and blessed and determinedly send all goodness and succor in life and beyond suffering and death that we can imagine and also the unimaginable inconceivable yet unfailingly realizable goodness and joy and utter relief that is all-envelopingly here and there and now and ever for every sensitive being throughout all universal buddhaverses!

About the Author

Robert Thurman is Professor Emeritus of Indo-Tibetan Buddhological Studies at Columbia University, Founder and Director of the American Institute of Buddhist Studies, and Co-Founder and President of Tibet House US/ Menla, His Holiness the Dalai Lama's Official Cultural Center in America, in service of the people of Tibet. A disciple and close friend of the Dalai Lama's for over 50 years, he is a leading worldwide lecturer on Tibetan Buddhism, passionate activist for the plight of the Tibetan people, skilled translator of Buddhist texts, and inspiring writer of popular Buddhist books. His recent book is the 300-page graphic novel *Man of Peace: The Illustrated Life Story of the Dalai Lama of Tibet*. Website: www.bobthurman.com.

In partnership with Nena, Ganden, and Uma Thurman, a dedicated staff, and wise and generous contributors, he now focuses on expanding Tibet House US and its Menla Retreat & Spa Resort in the Catskill mountains as an anchor center in the global network of Tibet House Centers for the preservation, promotion, study, and practice of the precious Tibetan Buddhist culture with its healing arts and sciences of body, mind, and spirit, dedicated as a complement to the vast life work of its founding patron, His Holiness the Dalai Lama.

Websites: www.tibethouse.us and www.menla.org.

Hay House Titles of Related Interest

YOU CAN HEAL YOUR LIFE, the movie,
starring Louise Hay & Friends
(available as a 1-DVD program, an expanded 2-DVD set,
and an online streaming video)
Learn more at www.hayhouse.com/louise-movie

THE SHIFT, the movie,
starring Dr. Wayne W. Dyer
(available as a 1-DVD program, an expanded 2-DVD set,
and an online streaming video)
Learn more at www.hayhouse.com/the-shift-movie

* * *

INTIMATE CONVERSATIONS WITH THE DIVINE:
Prayer, Guidance, and Grace, by Caroline Myss

THE LIFETIMES WHEN JESUS AND BUDDHA
KNEW EACH OTHER:
A History of Mighty Companions, by Gary R. Renard

THE TAO MADE EASY:
Timeless Wisdom to Navigate a Changing World, by Alan Cohen

TRUE SOURCE OF HEALING:
How the Ancient Tibetan Practice of Soul Retrieval Can Transform
and Enrich Your Life, by Tenzin Wangyal Rinpoche

All of the above are available at your local bookstore,
or may be ordered by contacting Hay House (see next page).

* * *

We hope you enjoyed this Hay House book. If you'd like to receive our online catalog featuring additional information on Hay House books and products, or if you'd like to find out more about the Hay Foundation, please contact:

Hay House, Inc., P.O. Box 5100, Carlsbad, CA 92018-5100
(760) 431-7695 or (800) 654-5126
(760) 431-6948 (fax) or (800) 650-5115 (fax)
www.hayhouse.com® • www.hayfoundation.org

———

Published in Australia by: Hay House Australia Pty. Ltd.,
18/36 Ralph St., Alexandria NSW 2015
Phone: 612-9669-4299 • *Fax:* 612-9669-4144
www.hayhouse.com.au

Published in the United Kingdom by: Hay House UK, Ltd.,
The Sixth Floor, Watson House, 54 Baker Street, London W1U 7BU
Phone: +44 (0)20 3927 7290 • *Fax:* +44 (0)20 3927 7291
www.hayhouse.co.uk

Published in India by: Hay House Publishers India,
Muskaan Complex, Plot No. 3, B-2, Vasant Kunj, New Delhi 110 070
Phone: 91-11-4176-1620 • *Fax:* 91-11-4176-1630
www.hayhouse.co.in

———

Access New Knowledge.
Anytime. Anywhere.

Learn and evolve at your own pace
with the world's leading experts.

www.hayhouseU.com